Argentina

Argentina

BY JEAN F. BLASHFIELD

Enchantment of the World™
Second Series

CHILDREN'S PRESS®

An Imprint of Scholastic Inc.

New York   Toronto   London   Auckland   Sydney
Mexico City   New Delhi   Hong Kong
Danbury, Connecticut

Frontispiece: **Church of St. Francis, Salta**

Consultant: Maria Victoria Murillo, Professor, Department of Political Science and the School of International and Public Affairs, Columbia University, New York, New York

Please note: All statistics are as up-to-date as possible at the time of publication.

Book production by The Design Lab

Library of Congress Cataloging-in-Publication Data
Blashfield, Jean F.
  Argentina / by Jean F. Blashfield.
      pages cm. — (Enchantment of the world)
  Previously published: 2007.
  Includes bibliographical references and index.
  Audience: Grades 4–6.
  ISBN 978-0-531-21250-9 (library binding)
  1. Australia—Juvenile literature. I. Title.
  F2808.2.B56 2015
  982—dc23   2014031836

1 2 3 4 5 6 7 8 9 10 R 24 23 22 21 20 19 18 17 16 15

Iguazú Falls

Contents

Left to right: **Harvesting grapes, herding sheep, sports fans, hiking at Mt. Aconcagua, boy playing soccer**

CHAPTER 1

A Land Like No Other

ARGENTINA IS A LAND OF SPECTACULARLY DIVERSE environments. It has vast, wind-blown plains, jagged mountain peaks, thundering falls, and desolate plateaus. There are slowly moving walls of ice, swampy wetlands, bright blue lakes, and sandy beaches by the mile. The country, which covers most of southern South America, boasts both the highest and the lowest points in the Americas.

Argentina also has an amazing variety of people. In the late 1800s and early 1900s, the nation had a booming economy that drew millions of immigrants from all around the world. People came from Italy, Poland, and Russia. They came

Opposite: **Spectacular Mount Fitz Roy lies in southern Argentina near the border with Chile. Its steep rock cliffs make it extraordinarily difficult to climb.**

ARGENTINA

- ● Cities of over 500,000 people
- ○ Other cities
- ✪ National capital

0 ——— 300 miles

0 ——— 300 kilometers

BOLIVIA

PARAGUAY

BRAZIL

Pozuelos Lake

Campo Durán

Tartagal

Pilcomayo R.

San Salvador de Jujuy

Salta

El Rey Nat'l Park

Iguazú National Park

Metán

Castelli

Pirané

San Miguel de Tucumán

Formosa

Belén

Resistencia

Posadas

Catamarca

Santiago del Estero

Corrientes

Uruguay R.

Chilecito

Frías

Goya

Santo Tomé

Talampaya National and Ischigualasto Provincial Park

La Paz

Paso de los Libres

Santa

San Juan

Córdoba

Rafaela

Fe

Paraná

El Palmar Nat'l Park

Quebrada del Condorito Nat'l Park

Rosario

Mendoza

Río Cuarto

Zárate

URUGUAY

San Luis

Pergamino

Mercedes

Junín

Tigre

Buenos Aires

San Rafael

La Plata

San Carlos de Bólivar

Lobos

Dolores

Santa Rosa

Ayacúcho

General Acha

Bahía

Juárez

Mar del Plata

Zapala

Neuquén

Blanca

Miramar

Necochea

Lanín National Park

Carmen de Patagones

Nahuel Huapi National Park

Los Arrayanes National Park

Viedma

San Carlos de Bariloche

Puerto Madryn

Esquel

Rawson

Comodoro Rivadavia

Caleta Olivia

Perito Moreno National Park

Los Glaciares National Park

Río Gallegos

Falkland Islands (United Kingdom)

Argentina

Río Turbio

Río Grande

Ushuaia

Tierra del Fuego National Park

PACIFIC OCEAN

CHILE

ATLANTIC OCEAN

N
W · E
S

A Guaraní man plays a drum in a village in Misiones Province in northeastern Argentina. Several thousand Guaraní people live in this part of Argentina.

from France, Germany, Japan, Wales, Holland, and Syria. They changed the look, feel, and sound of Argentina's cities, particularly the capital of Buenos Aires.

Argentina has had a long and sometimes troubled history. People have lived in the region for tens of thousands of years. Long ago, the native people farmed, hunted, and traded. Most died from disease and warfare following the Spanish invasion in the 1500s. After Argentina declared its independence in the early nineteenth century, civil war rocked the country. But by late in the century, the economy was strong, and the country was stable.

In the twentieth century, however, the country had faced many difficulties. Several times, the military overthrew democratically elected presidents. And in the 1970s, in what is

More tourists visit Buenos Aires than any other city in South America. People come from all over the world to enjoy its graceful architecture and bustling streets.

called the Dirty War, the country's military leaders tortured and killed thousands of people who opposed them. Democracy returned to Argentina in 1983, but by the end of the century the country's economy was collapsing. By 2002, Argentine money was worth practically nothing. In the years since, the country has struggled back to its feet. Farms are booming, cities are thriving, and tourists are traveling to Argentina to see the awe-inspiring landscapes.

Today, Argentina is a place of graceful neighborhoods, lively conversation, dramatic dances, and romantic cowboys. Come explore Argentina. It is a land like no other.

A cowboy herds sheep in southern Argentina. More than sixteen million sheep are raised on Argentina's mountains and plains.

CHAPTER 2

The Amazing Land

ARGENTINA IS THE EIGHTH-LARGEST COUNTRY IN the world, with a total area of 1,074,000 square miles (2,780,000 square kilometers). In that space is a fantastic array of land. There are mountains, deserts, plains, rain forests, glaciers, vast lakes, and long seashores.

The Lay of the Land

Argentina is a long triangle, shaped something like an ice cream cone with a little spoon sticking out of the top. That "spoon" is a curve of land that reaches northeastward between Paraguay and Uruguay to touch Brazil. The northwestern part of the cone borders Paraguay and Bolivia. The whole length of the western side of the cone, all the way to the tip, shares the Andes Mountains with Chile. Together, Chile and Argentina occupy Tierra del Fuego, a chain of islands, or archipelago, at the southern end of the continent. The eastern side of the ice cream cone is the Atlantic Ocean, a 3,100-mile (5,000 km) sweep of beaches, bays, and rocky coasts.

Argentina's Geographic Features

Area: 1,074,000 square miles (2,780,000 sq km)

Highest Point: Mount Aconcagua, 22,834 feet (6,960 m) above sea level

Lowest Point: Laguna del Carbón (Carbon Lake), 345 feet (105 m) below sea level

Longest River: Solely in Argentina: Salado, 710 miles (1,143 km)

Longest Border: With Chile, 3,200 miles (5,150 km)

Largest Lake: Argentino Lake, 566 square miles (1,466 sq km)

Highest Average Temperature: 90°F (32°C) in January in Mendoza region

Lowest Average Temperature: 27°F (−3°C) in July in southern Patagonia

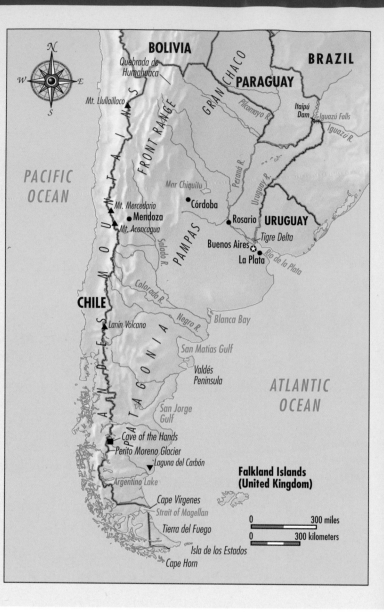

The North

Many rivers run through the northern part of Argentina. The Paraguay River serves as the border between Argentina and Paraguay. It is the main tributary of the Paraná River. The Uruguay River defines the border with Brazil and Uruguay in the northeast. It flows into the huge estuary called the Río de la Plata. An estuary is a bay where the saltwater from the ocean mingles with the freshwater carried by rivers emptying into it. The longest river completely within Argentina is the Salado. Starting in the northwest, it runs 710 miles (1,143 km) to join the Paraná River in the northeast.

Buenos Aires is located on the Río de la Plata. The physical size of the city has grown over the centuries because of the amount of soil brought down the Río de la Plata into the estuary. That soil is deposited in the estuary, especially on the south bank where Buenos Aires is located. As the soil accumulates, the land grows, and so does the city.

About one-quarter of the land in South America drains into the Río de la Plata.

Iguazú Falls is three times wider than Niagara Falls, which lies on the border between the United States and Canada. The name Iguazú comes from Guaraní words that mean "great water."

The area where Argentina, Brazil, and Paraguay meet is called the Triple Frontier. It is formed by the meeting of the Iguazú and Paraná Rivers. Along the border between Argentina and Brazil, the Iguazú River tumbles over horseshoe-shaped falls that extend for 1.7 miles (2.7 km). Iguazú Falls is considered one of the most spectacular waterfalls in the world.

The region between the Paraná and the Uruguay Rivers is called Mesopotamia, meaning "between the rivers" in Greek. Mesopotamia is among the lushest regions in Argentina. It is a land of swamps and heavy rainfall.

The Andes

The towering Andes mountain range stretches about 4,300 miles (7,000 km) north to south, across the full length of eastern South America, making it the longest mountain

Crunch!

The Andes Mountains were formed by the movement of giant pieces of the earth's outer layer of tectonic plates. As these plates collide, pushing against one another, the land crumples and is forced upward. These tectonic plates are still colliding, and the mountains are still slowly growing, with the land rising about 4 inches (10 centimeters) every one hundred years.

chain on earth. The name *Andes* probably comes from a word meaning "east" in the language of the Quechua people, an indigenous, or native, group in South America. The Andes run through seven countries—Venezuela, Colombia, Ecuador, Peru, Bolivia, Chile, and Argentina.

High and Low

Mount Aconcagua (left) means "Sentinel of Stone." It is the highest peak in Argentina and in the entire Western Hemisphere, reaching 22,834 feet (6,960 meters). The first person known to have reached the mountain's peak was a Swiss climber named Matthias Zurbriggen in 1897, but there is evidence that Incan people had climbed it much earlier. Mount Aconcagua is not actually part of the Andes Mountains. Instead, it is located in the Front Range, to the east of the Andes. The mountain has two summits, one 95 feet (29 m) higher than the other.

Patagonia, in southern Argentina, includes the lowest spot in the Western Hemisphere. Laguna del Carbón (Carbon Lake) is located 345 feet (105 m) below sea level in a canyon near the port of San Julian.

The highest peak in Argentina is Mount Aconcagua. Ojos del Salado, located on the Chile-Argentina border, is the world's highest volcano. It has two peaks, both reaching 22,615 feet (6,893 m) above sea level. It also has fumaroles, openings through which steam and gas escape. Ojos del Salado has not had a significant eruption in more than a thousand years. At least a dozen other volcanoes in Argentina are still active.

High in the Andes is a plateau area called the Altiplano (high plain). Most of it lies in Bolivia and Peru. In Argentina, it is called the Puna. This high plain—the world's largest

The towering Andes Mountains block clouds blowing across South America from the west. The clouds drop their rain on the western side of the Andes, leaving much of Argentina, including Salta Province in the northwestern part of the country, quite dry.

outside of Tibet in Asia—is about the size of the U.S. state of North Dakota. It has an average elevation of 12,300 feet (3,750 m). Rugged volcanoes and vast salt flats are found in the Puna. Though it is primarily a desert, the Puna has many lakes that are home to colorful flamingos and other birds.

For centuries, Argentine ranchers have grazed cattle on the vast grasslands of the Pampas.

The Pampas

The Pampas is a vast, mainly flat area of grasslands. Much of the region is covered with huge cattle ranches called *estancias*. The ranch lands are gradually being turned into croplands because the Pampas has some of the world's richest soil. The Pampas also includes a mountain range called the Pampas Hills. They are much smaller and lower than the Andes. They tend to be dry on the western slopes and wetter on the eastern slopes.

A tourist boat approaches Perito Moreno Glacier. The glacier is slowly pushing into Lake Argentino.

Patagonia

A region called Patagonia covers much of southern Argentina. Much of this area consists of barren plains dotted with lakes. The climate tends to be dry and cool. Though parts of Patagonia were long used for raising sheep, people rarely visited this part of Argentina. Then, in the twentieth century, oil was discovered there, and oil companies began building facilities. In the twen-

The Reappearing Town

Laguna Epecuén in southern Patagonia is one of the saltiest lakes in the world. For many years, the town of Villa Epecuén that developed near it was regarded as a health spa. Then, in the 1980s, a long period of heavy rains broke a nearby dam and the lake overflowed its banks and flooded the town. Not until 2009 did the water begin to recede, and the rotting remains of the town started to appear again.

tieth century, travelers began appreciating Patagonia's dramatic expanses, and now it has many hotels and tourist destinations.

In eastern Patagonia, near the Andes, massive sheets of ice called glaciers are common. Los Glaciares National Park features many glaciers moving slowly down the Andes. Footbridges cross Perito Moreno Glacier so that visitors can walk out and observe the impressive ice up close.

El Calafate, once a wool-trading town, has become the gateway to Los Glaciares National Park. In 2011, one clever businessman opened what he called the world's only bar made out of glacial ice. Customers are given warm capes and gloves to wear while inside the ice palace. The town also boasts a science museum called the Glaciarium, which features exhibits on the formation of the glaciers in the region.

Argentina's largest lake, Argentino Lake, lies within Los Glaciares National Park. Boats on the lake sometimes skim along the front of a glacier wall, while trying to keep out of the way of ice chunks that might break off and tumble down into the water at any moment. The lake is the source of the Santa Cruz River, which runs toward the Atlantic Ocean.

Tierra del Fuego

Patagonia ends at Cape Vírgenes, where Portuguese explorer Ferdinand Magellan stepped ashore in 1520. He and his men were the first Europeans to visit the region, and the water that separates the mainland from the group of islands called Tierra del Fuego is now called the Strait of Magellan. Magellan himself named the islands Tierra del Fuego, "Land of Fire," perhaps after seeing the campfires of native people along the shore.

Rugged ridges and valleys mark the land in Tierra del Fuego.

On a map of Antarctica, there's a long peninsula snaking off to the north. That peninsula and a triangle to the south of it extending all the way to the South Pole are regarded as part of Argentina. The first Argentine to travel to Antarctica was José María Sobral, in 1901. He was with a Swedish Antarctic expedition that was forced to spend two winters on the continent. A permanent Argentine scientific base called Orcadas was built on Laurie Island in 1904. It is the oldest base on the frozen continent.

Argentina now has several permanent scientific bases on the peninsula and nearby islands. The permanent population there is about two hundred. An icebreaker ship brings food and other supplies to the people. In 1978, an Argentine boy named Emilio Palama was born at one of these bases, making him the first person born on the continent of Antarctica.

Only the eastern third of the Tierra del Fuego archipelago belongs to Argentina. The rest of Tierra del Fuego belongs to Chile, which wraps around the bottom of Patagonia. The main island in the chain is the largest island in South America. Ushuaia, on the island of Tierra del Fuego, is the southernmost city in the world, and is the setting off point for many journeys to Antarctica. The trip from Ushuaia to Antarctica takes about two days by boat.

Climate

Argentina's seasons are the opposite of those in North America. When it is winter in the Northern Hemisphere, it is summer in Argentina. Argentine children go to school from March through mid-December, which is from autumn to spring. From mid-December until March they are on summer vacation.

Because it is such a long country, Argentina's climate changes with latitude, or the distance from the equator. People in the far north live with subtropical weather. Summers are very humid, with lots of precipitation spread evenly throughout the year. The frequent rain nourishes the lush plant growth in the forests. Buenos Aires is located farther south and has a milder climate. In January, the city experiences average high temperatures of 84 degrees Fahrenheit (29 degrees Celsius), while in July the average high is 57°F (14°C). The western part of the Pampas grasslands is dry, while the north is warmer and gets more rain. Winters are fairly mild, but it often snows in the southern Pampas. The winters in Patagonia feature snow and frigid temperatures. Tierra del Fuego can get snow even in summer, when the temperature rarely rises above 48°F (9°C). Most of the islands are too cold for trees to grow.

Spectacular Spikes of Andean Snow

Above 13,000 feet (about 4,000 m) in the dryer parts of the Andes Mountains, snow can form into startling spikes several feet high. These spikes, called *penitentes*, are formed by a process called sublimation. When it snows, the hot sun at such high altitudes can turn the snow directly into water vapor, without melting it into water first. Some areas sublimate faster than others. This leaves thin, towering spikes of snow between low areas where a lot of the snow has sublimated.

Looking at Argentina's Cities

Buenos Aires is the capital of Argentina and its largest city, with a population of 2,890,151 in 2010. More than 13 million people live in the Buenos Aires metropolitan area, accounting for about one-third of the country's total population.

With a population of 1,329,604, Córdoba is the nation's second-largest city as well as its educational center and the heart of the agricultural Pampas. Thousands of young people are drawn to its seven universities, including the nation's oldest, the National University of Córdoba (below), founded in 1613. Much of the architecture is from the early years of the city.

Manufacturing, especially of airplanes, cars, and agricultural machinery, is important in Córdoba.

Rosario, located northwest of Buenos Aires on the banks of the Paraná River, is the third-largest city, home to 1,193,605. It has a long, welcoming beach-filled waterfront called *la costanera*. Both a port and a railway center, Rosario is an important center for shipping agricultural products. Industry is also growing in the area around Rosario.

Mendoza (above), the nation's fourth-largest city, has a population of about 957,000. Mendoza is surrounded by the largest wine-growing area in Latin America. Although the city is subject to high temperatures and humidity, a wealth of trees keeps people comfortable. A light-rail line going throughout the city opened in 2012.

La Plata, the nation's fifth-largest city, has a population of 654,324. It is located in the northern Pampas on the banks of the Río de la Plata about 35 miles (56 km) from Buenos Aires. The city's cathedral is the largest in Argentina, and the National University of La Plata is widely known for teaching sciences. The city's industries include meatpacking and chemical manufacturing.

CHAPTER 3

Incredible Life

ARGENTINA HAS A GREAT DIVERSITY OF HABITAT, from humid jungles in the north to towering glaciers in the far south. Because of this, the country is home to an astonishing variety of living things.

Opposite: **Toucans use their large bills to reach hanging fruit and explore deep holes in trees, in search of food.**

Birds

Argentina is alive with birds. Perhaps as many as a thousand species can be seen there, drawing bird-watchers from all over the world. Some of the birds blend in with their surroundings, while others are so colorful that they compete with the flowers of the jungle.

Toucans, which have wildly oversized brightly colored beaks, live in northern Argentina. Many species of parrots, parakeets, and macaws also brighten the trees. Less color-ful birds include the rufous hornero, a kind of ovenbird. Ovenbirds earned their name because their round, clay nests resemble old outdoor ovens.

Rheas usually live in open areas. If predators approach, rheas escape by running.

Argentina is also home to herons and hawks, woodpeckers, pelicans, and more than thirty species of hummingbirds. A rare duck called the Brazilian merganser lives in northeastern Argentina. Almost extinct, there may be fewer than 250 of these birds in the wild, mostly in Brazil.

Running across the open grasslands of Argentina are flightless birds that look rather like the African ostrich. They are called *ñandus* in Argentina, and rheas elsewhere. They can't fly, but

Flying High

The Andean condor, one of Argentina's national symbols, is the largest flying land bird in the Western Hemisphere. These black and white vultures have wingspans of up to 10 feet (3 m). Andean condors often live high in the mountains. They soar, hardly ever flapping their wings. The birds are protected in Quebrada del Condorito National Park in the central part of the country.

they run rapidly with a great flapping of wings. On the Pampas, they have been known to charge gauchos on horseback.

The world's biggest colony of Magellanic penguins is located at Punta Tombo, a small peninsula along the coast in Patagonia. In the past, the penguin population there has been about four hundred thousand, but in recent years young chicks have been facing greater dangers. The seas have been growing warmer, which produces heavier rains that the chicks cannot survive. In addition, some of the fish that the penguins eat are swimming farther out to sea to find the cooler temperatures that they enjoy. As the chicks' food supply diminishes, some of them starve to death.

Magellanic penguins mate for life. The female usually lays two eggs. Both the male and female keep the eggs warm, and both care for and feed the chicks after they are born.

Long-Distance Travelers

Speckled shorebirds called red knots make one of the longest migrations of any bird on the planet. They breed in the Arctic, in the northern polar region, and then migrate south. Some go all the way to Tierra del Fuego, at South America's southern tip. That's a 9,000-mile (15,000 km) journey. During their travels, these birds stop in Delaware Bay, in the mid-Atlantic section of the United States, where they feed on the eggs of horseshoe crabs. In the early 2000s, the number of red knots shrank, in large part because people were harvesting more horseshoe crabs, so the red knots did not have as much food. To protect the red knots, government agencies in the United States changed the season when horseshoe crabs can be caught, and the birds' numbers are no longer dropping.

Mammals

Many types of wild cats live in Argentina. The largest is the jaguar, which sometimes grows 6 feet (2 m) long and weighs as much as 350 pounds (160 kilograms). Another large Argentine cat, the puma, lives throughout the Western Hemisphere, and is sometimes called the mountain lion or the cougar. Pampas cats are smaller and have reddish-brown stripes broken into spots. They are sometimes raised as pets, though they are still wild.

Most of Argentina's mammals are rodents. The soft-furred viscacha looks like part squirrel and part rabbit. Even more rabbit-like is the Patagonian mara, which is actually a relative of the guinea pig. The capybara is the world's largest rodent, which sometimes grows as much as 4 feet (1.2 m) long.

Capybaras are herbivores, and are often seen in large groups grazing on grasses or water plants. Capybaras are hunted for both their meat and their skins, which make excellent leather.

Capybaras live near water. They have webbed feet that help them swim.

Big Cat

South America's biggest cat, the jaguar, is a top predator, meaning no other animal hunts it. Jaguars ambush prey, rather than chase it down. They move quietly through the forest and then leap onto prey. Jaguars have an incredibly powerful bite and can bite through a turtle's shell or an armadillo's body.

Jaguars are becoming increasingly rare. They used to live throughout South America, but they have declined because of hunting and habitat destruction, as their forest homes have been cut down. In Argentina, they are now limited to only three known populations, all in the north. Argentina declared this majestic cat a natural national monument in 2001. Many organizations are working to start new populations in other areas where these cats can be protected from humans.

Incredible Life **33**

The Trouble with Beavers

In Tierra del Fuego, a rodent from North America is causing damage. In 1946, twenty beavers were introduced into the area from Canada to start a new industry using beaver fur. The industry failed, but the beavers kept breeding. Today, there are an estimated one hundred thousand beavers in the region. The beavers fell trees to build dams and make ponds. They have damaged half the forests along rivers in Tierra del Fuego and have moved into Patagonia and the Pampas, where they lay waste to the countryside. Unlike many tree species in North America, trees native to southern Argentina don't revive after being gnawed on by beavers. The governments of Argentina and Chile are trying to get rid of the beavers. They have tried blowing up the beaver dams and paying hunters to trap the animals. So far, nothing has helped.

Argentina is home to a small number of monkeys, including capuchins and howler monkeys. The large howler monkeys make one of the most distinctive noises in Argentina's northern forests. These monkeys move in groups through the treetops and communicate by loud, echoing calls, especially at dawn and dusk. Night monkeys, also called owl monkeys, are much quieter. They have large eyes for seeing during their nighttime ramblings.

One of the largest mammals in Argentina is the giant anteater. Curled up in its long, narrow head is a sticky tongue that may be up to 2 feet (60 centimeters) long, in a body that sometimes reaches 7 feet (2 m) in length. The giant anteater has powerful claws that it uses to break up rock-hard termite nests. The giant armadillo, found only in northern Argentina, also consumes termites. This armored mammal sometimes grows 5 feet (1.5 m) long, from its nose to the tip of its tail.

The only marsupials, or pouched mammals, in Argentina are four species of mouse opossums. They are much smaller than North American opossums and tend to live in trees.

Argentina's lengthy coastline is home to, or at least visited by, many sea mammals. Right whales and killer whales can be seen offshore, and the shore itself is visited by sea lions, fur seals, and elephant seals.

Southern right whales are huge but agile. Although they can be 50 feet (15 m) long, they frequently leap out of the water, a practice called breaching.

Plant Life

The types of plants that grow in Argentina vary greatly from region to region. Parts of northern Argentina feature rich rain forests filled with laurel, cedar, and many other trees. The lower slopes of the Andes support both evergreen and deciduous forests. El Rey National Park in the southern Andes protects a cloud forest, which is a rain forest located high on a mountain where clouds linger. This is the perfect habitat for many orchids and the tough-leaved bromeliads, which sometimes live on tree branches rather than rooting in the ground.

Horses make their way through the mossy rain forest at El Rey National Park.

Small shrubs and grasses grow in the dry Puna region, and much of the Pampas is covered with scrubland where acacia, mimosa, and ombu trees are mixed with tall grasses. The Pampas grass gets its name from the Pampas region. It has tall leaves with sharp edges and beautiful, feathery flowers that rise up from among the leaves. Dry grasslands and deserts also cover much of Patagonia. Beech and cypress thrive in the river valleys of Tierra del Fuego.

Pampas grass grows in clumps. The feathery stalks often reach 10 feet (3 m) tall.

Symbols of a Nation

Argentina's national tree is the ceibo, a small tree that grows near rivers and in wetlands. During the summer, it produces clusters of gorgeous, vivid red blossoms. These blossoms are the national flower of Argentina.

National Parks and Monuments

Argentina has established twenty-five national parks and several natural monuments as part of an effort to protect its extraordinary landscapes, plants, and animals. Nahuel Huapi National Park (right), the nation's oldest national park, was established in 1934. Located in the foothills of the Andes, it features glaciers, waterfalls, thick forests, and rushing rivers. One of the many animal species found there is the pudu, a deer so small that it looks more like a rodent. It stands no more than 15 inches (38 cm) high at the shoulder.

Pozuelos Lake is a natural monument high in the Andes that protects many waterbirds and the vicuña, the smallest camel relative. The vicuña is nocturnal, so visitors to the park rarely see it. El Palmar National Park in the northeast protects the rare Yatay palm trees, which sometimes live to be eight hundred years old.

Life Long Ago

Many paleontologists, scientists who study fossils, spend time searching for the remains of dinosaurs in Argentina, where many fantastic discoveries have been made. In 1987, fossils were discovered in Patagonia from a previously unknown type of dinosaur. Scientists named it *Argentinosaurus*. The giant creature was a plant-eater, probably 117 feet (35 m) long. Another new type of dinosaur, *Futalognkosaurus*, was found in Patagonia in 2000. It was at least 100 feet (30 m) long. Talampaya National Park, an area of high red-stone canyons in a dry area east of the Andes, has been the site of many dinosaur fossil discoveries. Far north in Salta, dinosaur fossils are also found in Los Cardones National Park.

Many ancient fossils, such as this reptile relative that lived ninety million years ago, have been found in Patagonia.

Paleontologists have also unearthed fossils of other kinds of creatures in Patagonia. In 2003, they found fossils of a snake that dates to nearly 100 million years ago, making it the oldest snake fossil ever discovered. This snake shows remnants of legs, indicating that it evolved from a legged creature. Paleontologists think that this fossil is evidence that snakes evolved on land, not in the sea as previously believed.

The Biggest Dinosaur

The largest dinosaur ever found was discovered in 2011 by a farmworker in a desert in Patagonia. The giant creature was about 130 feet (40 m) long—longer than three full-size buses parked behind one another—and as tall as a seven-story building. It weighed about 170,000 pounds (77 metric tons), as much as fourteen African elephants. In comparison, a *Tyrannosaurus rex* probably weighed only about 15,000 pounds (6.8 metric tons). This immense plant-eater roamed about 95 to 100 million years ago, when the region was forested. Scientists have not yet named this monumental dinosaur.

CHAPTER 4

The Story of Argentina

SCIENTISTS ARE NOT CERTAIN WHEN HUMANS FIRST moved into South America. Recent discoveries show that it may have been thirty thousand years ago. Evidence suggests that humans hunted giant sloths, or *Megatherium*, at that time. The first fossils of those now-extinct elephant-sized animals were found in Argentina in 1788. Their skeletons were the largest ancient animals known until dinosaurs were discovered.

Opposite: **More than eight hundred hands are painted on the walls of the Cave of the Hands. The cave also has paintings of animals, people, hunting scenes, and zigzag patterns.**

The Original People

Among the oldest evidence of the ancient indigenous peoples that occupied Argentina is a cave in western Patagonia called the Cave of the Hands. Paintings on the walls have been dated to 9,300 years ago. Most of the paintings, which are in many colors, are of hands, and most of the hands are left hands, which indicates that most of these people were right-handed.

The Yaghan people traditionally lived by hunting and gathering wild plants.

At first, the humans who occupied South America were hunter-gatherers, moving with the seasons to hunt food and seek shelter. Gradually, the huge mammals they hunted disappeared, and they began to realize that the seeds of some plants could be collected and planted again the following year. By

From Australia to Tierra del Fuego?

Scientists have long thought that Asians migrated across the Bering Strait into what is now Alaska and spread southward from there, populating both North and South America. But now they are finding evidence that there were humans in South America long before they could have migrated from the north. There are signs that humans lived on Tierra del Fuego as much as thirty thousand years ago. And the modern science of genetics has shown that South American native peoples may have ancestors in common with indigenous peoples in Australia and the Pacific islands. Some of these peoples may have crossed the ocean by boat—perhaps from Australia—long before early native peoples spread throughout North America. Scientists need to discover more before they can solve the mystery of South America's ancient human history.

about seven thousand years ago, some indigenous peoples were creating farming settlements. These settlements were mostly in the north, where water could support crops.

Over the centuries, the number of people grew, and they began to separate into groups that occupied different areas and developed different cultures, languages, and lifestyles. Peoples in the north such as the Guaraní and the Charrúa were farmers. Their main crops were corn and a root called cassava. Farther south were the Querandí, who were renowned for their hunting skills. They used weapons such as bows and arrows or *boleadoras* (stones connected by strips of leather) to hunt animals such as deer and ñandus. The Mapuche, a group of related peoples, lived in parts of Patagonia. They farmed, and the women made textiles that were valuable trade goods. Groups in the south, such as the Selknam and the Yaghan, hunted sea lions, shellfish, and other creatures.

European Exploration

When Italian explorer Christopher Columbus arrived in the Americas in 1492, he was trying to reach Asia. But there were two continents in the way,

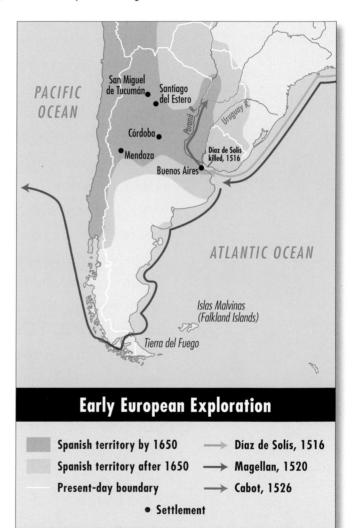

Early European Exploration

▨ Spanish territory by 1650	→ Díaz de Solís, 1516
▨ Spanish territory after 1650	→ Magellan, 1520
▔ Present-day boundary	→ Cabot, 1526
• Settlement	

PACIFIC OCEAN

San Miguel de Tucumán
Santiago del Estero
Córdoba
Mendoza
Buenos Aires
Paraná R.
Uruguay R.
Díaz de Solís killed, 1516

ATLANTIC OCEAN

Islas Malvinas (Falkland Islands)

Tierra del Fuego

continents that came to be called North and South America. Still hoping to reach Asia, Spaniard Juan Díaz de Solís sought a water route to Asia. In 1516, he discovered a wide estuary, an area where a river flows into the sea, and claimed the lands around the river for Spain. He himself didn't live to tell the Spanish king of his discovery because he was killed by native people he met onshore. The sailors on Díaz de Solís's ship carried word of the area back to Europe.

A few years later, in 1526, explorer Sebastian Cabot, an Englishman working for Spain, spent several months investigating the big estuary. Today, that river, which he named Río de la Plata, meaning "River of Silver," is part of the eastern border of Argentina. Cabot supplied a small fort built on the Paraná River, which feeds into the estuary. Though it did not last, it was the first Spanish settlement in Argentina.

In 1536, Pedro de Mendoza and several Spanish families came to Argentina to stay. They founded a settlement on the south shore of the Río de la Plata. Mendoza named his settlement Santa María del Buen Aire, which means "Holy Mary of the Fair Winds." This was soon shortened to "Fair Winds," or Buenos Aires. After two years, the Spaniards abandoned the settlement following repeated attacks by indigenous people. It was another forty years before the settlement was rebuilt in the same spot, this time for good.

At the same time, Europeans were coming from the north, where Spanish soldiers called *conquistadores*, meaning "conquerors," had conquered the Inca Empire in Peru. They founded Santiago del Estero in 1553, making it the oldest

continuously occupied city in Argentina. They also founded other cities, including Mendoza, Tucumán, and Córdoba.

Buenos Aires was founded for the second time in 1580 by a Spanish conquistador named Juan de Garay.

Missionaries Arrive

About 1585, missionaries from Spain arrived in the region. They believed that the indigenous people should be gathered into communities called missions. They were to be turned into Christians, whether they wanted to be or not. The native people were to serve as labor for the missions. In some cases, the native men were armed and trained as militias to fight the soldiers of other colonial powers in the area, such as the Portuguese. For the most part, however, the Spaniards treated the native people poorly. Over the next century, most of them died of diseases introduced by the Europeans, or were killed.

As the numbers of indigenous people dropped, the Spaniards in the region no longer had a free source of labor. So they welcomed the slave ships that began to appear in Buenos Aires in the early 1700s. Slavery began to be abolished in 1813 but was not completely abolished until 1861.

Becoming a Nation

The Spanish king created a huge colony in South America in 1776 called the Viceroyalty of Río de la Plata. This viceroyalty included the lands that are now Argentina, Uruguay, Paraguay, Bolivia, and northern Chile. The viceroyalty's capital was Buenos Aires.

Spanish officials paid little attention to the Viceroyalty of Río de la Plata, especially after Spain entered a war against France in the early 1800s. During this period, the British navy ruled the seas. British ships brought troops to Argentina in 1806 to invade the viceroyalty and try to wrest it from Spanish control. The British failed at this time, and again the following year. After having fended off Britain, the Argentines began thinking of independence for themselves.

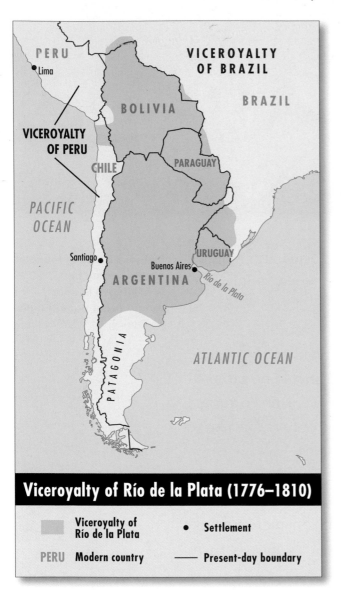

Viceroyalty of Río de la Plata (1776–1810)

| | Viceroyalty of Río de la Plata | • | Settlement |
| PERU | Modern country | —— | Present-day boundary |

On May 25, 1810, in what is known as the May Revolution, the leaders of Buenos Aires declared that they no longer owed allegiance to Spain. Royalists supporting the Spanish king, however, fought those who wanted to be independent. Then, in 1813, Uruguay declared its independence from the Viceroyalty of Río de la Plata. The larger portion of the viceroyalty declared its own independence on July 9, 1816, as the new nation of Argentina.

José de San Martín is considered one of the great liberators of South America.

The major influence in that move toward independence was José de San Martín, often called the Knight of the Andes. Though born in Argentina, he grew up in Spain and served in its army until becoming discontented with Spain ruling his native land. He returned to Argentina and took control of an army of revolutionaries. Cowboys from the Pampas called gauchos helped in the fight. San Martín's army succeeded in its quest to free the Río de la Plata region from Spain. Instead of remaining in Argentina, he and

The Gauchos

Like cowboys in American history and legend, the gauchos of Argentina are figures of both reality and fantasy. They were the descendants of Spanish men and indigenous women. Because they were often not welcome in cities, they tended to stay out on the Pampas, where they became known as great wranglers of cattle and horses.

The gauchos fought against the Spanish troops during the Argentine War of Independence. Their leader was General Martín Miguel de Güemes, the governor of Salta Province. He became a folk hero after he was shot in the back by royalist forces, ultimately dying from his wounds.

The traditional gaucho was a great horseman, and his horse was often the only thing he owned. He is often depicted wearing baggy trousers tucked into his boots. A gaucho carried an elaborately carved knife called a *facón*. When pursuing horses or cattle, he used a *boleadora*. This consisted of three stones or metal balls wrapped in leather and connected by leather thongs. The gaucho whirled the boleadora over his head and threw it at the legs of a running animal, bringing it down to the ground.

his troops marched across the Andes where they succeeded in also liberating Chile and Peru from Spanish rule.

Federalist troops working for Juan Manuel de Rosas wore red clothing and had large mustaches.

Power Struggle

San Martín did not leave behind a settled country. Instead, a civil war erupted between two Argentine groups—the Unitarists and the Federalists. The Unitarists wanted a strong central government. The Federalists were landowners who wanted the different regions to have their own strong governments, with a weak central government. In 1829, Federalist troops under Juan Manuel de Rosas took control of Buenos Aires.

Rosas became Argentina's first powerful dictator, though certainly not the last. He was overthrown in 1852 when an army led by Justo José de Urquiza defeated his forces. Urquiza was helped by troops from Brazil and Uruguay. He

Justo José de Urquiza had once been close to Juan Manuel de Rosas, but in 1852 he rebelled against Rosas and defeated him at the Battle of Caseros.

put together a legislature, which drew up Argentina's first constitution in 1853. The country was divided into large parts called provinces. The constitution created a new organization of provinces called a confederation. Buenos Aires separated briefly as the State of Buenos Aires.

The confederation tried to succeed, but Buenos Aires refused to recognize its authority. By 1862, Argentines were ready to try something else. They formed a new national government with a new president, but many years would go by before the provinces came to accept that Buenos Aires would always have the greatest power in the country.

In a long-running battle with the indigenous people of Patagonia, Buenos Aires gradually established total control over the distant lands. In this campaign, called the Conquest of the Desert, Argentine forces ousted the native people and turned the land over to Europeans.

Argentine forces also fought against neighboring nations. From 1865 to 1870, Argentina, Brazil, and Uruguay combined forces against Paraguay, which was trying to acquire land that would give it a port. What is known as the War of the Triple Alliance became the deadliest war in Latin American history. By the time it was over, more than 60 percent of the population of Paraguay had died. Instead of gaining territory, Paraguay was forced to give up the land that is now much of Misiones, Chaco, and Formosa Provinces in Argentina.

The War of the Triple Alliance was the deadliest conflict in South American history. At least four hundred thousand people died during the war.

Growth and Change

Beginning in 1880 under the rule of General Julio Roca, the Argentine economy began growing rapidly. This attracted waves of immigrants from Europe. More than three million Europeans moved to Argentina between 1875 and 1914. At the time, this influx of immigrants was second only to the numbers entering the United States. It completely changed the flavor of Buenos Aires, giving it the air of a European city.

Some of the most powerful people in the country were the great landowners in the Pampas. They oversaw huge ranches, or *estancias*, where cattle were raised. Because of the

The massive Immigrants' Hotel was built at the port in Buenos Aires in the early twentieth century to handle new arrivals. The dining room could hold a thousand people at a time.

A police officer directs traffic in Buenos Aires in the early twentieth century. By this time, Buenos Aires was a thriving city.

importance of cattle, the great landowners became the most important people in Argentina. Together, the businesspeople and landowners worked to maintain power.

In 1912, the public finally protested its lack of a voice in the government. The president was forced to establish universal male voting by secret ballot. When Hipólito Yrigoyen was elected president in 1916, he became the first leader in South America to be elected by universal male suffrage (the right to vote). Yrigoyen kept Argentina out of World War I, which made him very popular. He served from 1916 to 1922 and again from 1928 to 1930. A former teacher, he helped improve the living conditions of the many poor people, and introduced public education.

Celebrating soldiers hold up pictures of General José Félix Uriburu immediately after the coup that drove Hipólito Yrigoyen from power.

Until 1930, Argentina had a line of successfully elected governments. Then, the worldwide economic downturn called the Great Depression began, and a military group, or *junta*, under José Félix Uriburu removed Yrigoyen from office. This was the first military coup, or takeover, in Argentina. Such takeovers would happen four more times in the twentieth century, in 1943, 1955, 1962, and 1976.

The Perón Years

As in World War I, Argentina remained neutral in World War II, in part because President Ramón S. Castillo wanted to continue trading with both sides in the conflict. The army overthrew Castillo in 1943. A series of generals took charge until Colonel Juan Perón won the presidential election in 1946. Unlike most previous leaders of Argentina, Perón tried to help working people rather than just the powerful. He improved wages and working conditions, controlled rents, and established maternity and vacation leave, social security, and health insurance. Perón was reelected in 1952 and, as president, worked to increase his own power.

By the early 1950s, Perón had antagonized the Roman Catholic Church by trying to limit its influence in politics. Perón's attitude toward the church made enemies of some army officers. In 1955, he was forced from office in a coup. He fled to Spain, where he lived for the next eighteen years.

Catholics gather in a square in Buenos Aires in 1955 to protest Juan Perón's policies.

Juan and Evita Perón

Juan Perón (1895–1974) was a native of Lobos, near Buenos Aires, but he spent his childhood in the harsh lands of Patagonia. He was accepted in the military academy at sixteen and remained a soldier his entire life, though he was always better known for his political skills than his military prowess. In the 1930s, he went to Europe where he observed firsthand the tactics of Italy's dictator, Benito Mussolini, and he gained some sympathy for the Nazi government of Germany, led by Adolf Hitler.

On his return to Argentina, he took part in a plot to overthrow President Ramón Castillo. The military coup was successful, and Perón gradually gained popularity among working-class people by instituting reforms that bettered their lives. In 1945, his story became forever

entwined with that of his wife, a singer and dancer named María Eva Duarte, who is better known as Evita. She supported the rights of the poor and became an immensely popular figure, especially after she persuaded the government to grant the vote to women. She made her husband more popular than ever. Evita Perón died in 1952.

On June 16, 1955, naval and air force officers bombed the government palace, hoping to kill Juan Perón. Instead, about three hundred people in the plaza near the palace were killed. Three months later, the military seized power, and Perón went into exile. He returned to Argentina in 1973, won the presidency once again, but died the following year. Today, Juan and Evita Perón remain tremendously popular among the people of Argentina.

In 1973, a Peronist named Hector Cámpora was elected president. A few months later he resigned so that Perón could return from exile and run for president. Perón won a resounding victory. His then wife, Isabel Martínez de Perón, became the vice president. Juan Perón died in July 1974, and his wife became president. However, she was unable to control any of the factions in Argentina. The military took over again in 1976.

Isabel Perón became president of Argentina in 1974. She was the first woman in any nation in the world to become president.

The Dirty War

After ousting Isabel Perón in 1976, a small group of military officers established a new government. They dissolved the national congress and ruled by terror. During the seven years they were in control, thousands of people were jailed and tortured. The military leaders announced that violence was necessary to keep the country stable. Anyone who protested

Finding the Disappeared

When no one did anything about the people who disappeared during the Dirty War, their mothers began to gather in Plaza de Mayo in front of the presidential palace every Thursday to demand action. Azucena Villaflor de Vincenti was the founder of Mothers of the Plaza de Mayo. This is a group of mothers who are still demanding answers to what happened to the Disappeared. She and several other women were murdered in 1977.

A group called the Grandmothers of the Plaza de Mayo has also searched for answers to the fate of the Disappeared. Pregnant women who were jailed during the Dirty War were allowed to give birth before they were killed. The Grandmothers are working to locate the babies, now adults, who were born to Disappeared mothers. More than one hundred of those adults have been found. Many more remain to be tracked down.

just quietly disappeared, and the graves of these people have never been found. Many of those who disappeared were the scientists and thinkers who should have led Argentina into the future. This terrible period has been called the Dirty War, and the many missing people are called the Disappeared.

When it was clear that the military authorities were losing the support of the people—because of their brutality and the poor economy—they came up with a way to get the Argentines to think about something else. In 1982, Argentina invaded a group of islands about 300 miles (480 km) off the southern tip of Patagonia. These islands, which the British called the Falklands and the Argentines called the Malvinas, had been controlled by Britain since 1833. When British troops arrived, unprepared Argentine troops quickly lost the conflict. More than 630 Argentine soldiers died. This loss caused the collapse of the military dictatorship. The president who had been acting for the military was forced to call for a real election.

An Uneasy Democracy

Raúl Alfonsín was elected president in 1983. He agreed to arrest and try officials responsible for the Disappeared. But very quickly it became clear that the military would oust him from office if he did not stop the trials. He was forced to

British troops roll through Stanley, the capital of the Falkland Islands, during the Falkland Islands War. Argentine troops occupied the town for two months during the war.

resign anyway because the economy was collapsing. Inflation was spiraling out of control. Millions of Argentines could no longer pay their rent or even buy food.

In 1989, Argentines elected Carlos Saúl Menem president to try to get the economy back on track. Menem altered trade rules, privatized many state-owned companies, and encouraged other nations to make new loans to the country. However, the people in the countryside suffered deepening poverty, and the slums in the cities expanded. In time, inflation slowed. Menem, who was reelected in 1995, left office in 1999.

Carlos Menem (in light suit) was very popular during his presidency.

Menem was followed by Fernando de la Rúa. In 2001, he cut spending on social programs and limited the amount of money that individuals could withdraw from the bank. People took to the streets in protest, and de la Rúa resigned. The following year, the value of the Argentine currency collapsed. Suddenly the Argentines' money was worth next to nothing. Many businesses failed, driving more people out of work.

In the years since, the economy has grown, and millions of new jobs have been created. President Cristina Fernández de Kirchner, who was first elected president in 2007, is working to repay the foreign nations that lost money in the 2002 collapse of the economy. Although Argentina has had a sometimes troubling past, with its growing economy, it has a promising future.

In 2001, demonstrators took to the streets of Argentine cities day after day to protest the country's economic policies.

CHAPTER 5

Governing a Nation

THE OFFICIAL NAME OF ARGENTINA IS THE ARGENTINE Republic (*República Argentina*). This name dates back to Argentina's constitution of 1853. That constitution was based largely on the U.S. Constitution. It declared Argentina a federal democracy. In a federal system, the different parts of the country—the provinces—agree to give up certain powers to a central government.

Argentine law requires everyone between the ages of eighteen and seventy to vote. In 2012, Argentina lowered the voting age from eighteen to sixteen, but people under age eighteen are not required to vote. Women have had the vote since 1949.

Opposite: **The Argentine National Congress meets in a grand building constructed in the early twentieth century.**

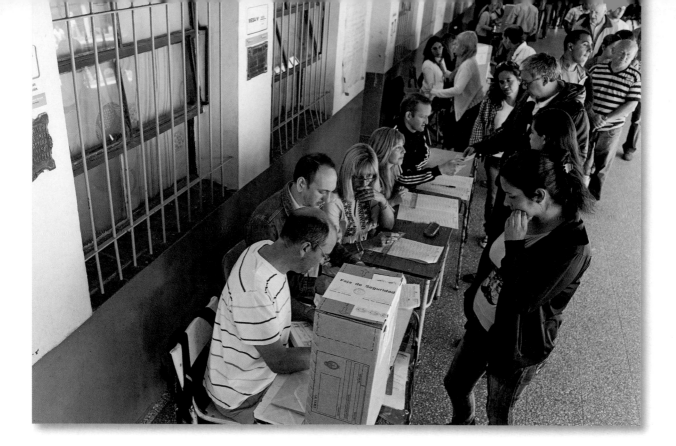

Argentines stand in line to vote during an election in 2013. Voting is compulsory in Argentina. People who do not vote could be fined.

The Federal Government

Argentina's government consists of three branches: executive, legislative, and judicial. The president is head of the executive branch, the branch that carries out the laws. The president and vice president are elected directly by the people to four-year terms and may serve two terms in a row. The various departments of the executive branch are run by cabinet ministers whom the president appoints.

The legislative, or lawmaking, branch of government in Argentina has two parts, or houses. The upper house is called the Senate. It has seventy-two seats, with each of the twenty-three provinces plus the Federal District electing three senators. Two of the senators from each province must represent the

major political party of that province. The third must come from the second-largest political party. Senators serve six-year terms, and one-third of them come up for election every two

The Argentine Senate debates a bill.

years. There are no limits on the number of terms they can serve. The lower house is called the Chamber of Deputies. It has 257 seats divided equally among the population of the nation. Deputies serve four-year terms, with one-half of the seats up for election every two years. The law requires that at least one-third of the members of congress be women.

Argentina's judicial branch is headed by the Supreme Court, which has five judges. These judges are appointed by the president and must be approved by at least two-thirds of the Senate. Below the Supreme Court are appellate courts

Ricardo Lorenzetti (center), the president of the Argentine Supreme Court, and his colleagues listen to testimony. The president of the court is chosen by its members.

National Government of Argentina

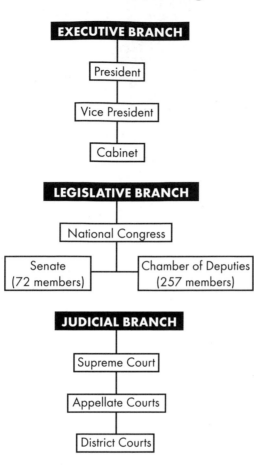

EXECUTIVE BRANCH

President

Vice President

Cabinet

LEGISLATIVE BRANCH

National Congress

Senate
(72 members)

Chamber of Deputies
(257 members)

JUDICIAL BRANCH

Supreme Court

Appellate Courts

District Courts

and district courts. Decisions made in district courts can be reviewed by the appellate courts. The judges in lower courts are appointed by the president.

The Military

The Argentina military consists of the army, navy, and air force. They are part of the Ministry of Defense, which is run

The National Anthem

The national anthem of Argentina is "¡Oíd, Mortales!" ("Hear, O Mortals!"). The lyrics were written by Vicente López y Planes as "*Marcha patriótica*" for music by Blas Parera. It was adopted as the national anthem in 1813 and modernized, with its newer name, in 1924.

Spanish lyrics

Oíd, mortales, el grito sagrado:
¡Libertad! ¡Libertad! ¡Libertad!
Oíd el ruido de rotas cadenas
Ved en trono a la noble igualdad.
Ya su trono dignísimo abrieron
Las Provincias Unidas del Sud
Y los libres del mundo responden:
¡Al gran pueblo argentino, salud!
¡Al gran pueblo argentino, salud!
Y los libres del mundo responden:
¡Al gran pueblo argentino, salud!

CHORUS
Sean eternos los laureles,
Que supimos conseguir.
Coronados de gloria vivamos,
¡O juremos con gloria morir!

English translation

Mortals! Hear the sacred cry;
Freedom! Freedom! Freedom!
Hear the noise of broken chains.
See noble Equality enthroned.
The United Provinces of the South
Have now displayed their worthy throne.
And the free peoples of the world reply:
We salute the great people of Argentina!
We salute the great people of Argentina!
And the free peoples of the world reply:
We salute the great people of Argentina!

CHORUS
May the laurels be eternal
That we knew how to win.
Let us live crowned with glory,
Or swear to die gloriously.

by civilians. The Ministry of the Interior oversees the border police and the coast guard. Military service is voluntary, and there are fewer than seventy-five thousand troops in the Argentina military. Argentina has sent soldiers to participate in United Nations peacekeeping operations, with Argentine soldiers and police serving in such places as Guatemala, Western Sahara, Angola, and Kosovo.

Beyond the Federal Government

Argentina is divided into twenty-three provinces. Buenos Aires, the national capital, is an autonomous, or self-governing, city, and has the same status as a province. Like U.S.

Members of the Argentine military march through Buenos Aires during an Independence Day celebration.

The Flag

The Argentine flag has three equal horizontal bands, with light blue on the top and bottom and white in between. On the center of the white band is the Sun of May, a radiant yellow sun with a human face. It is a replica of the design on Argentina's first coin, issued in 1813, recognizing the May Revolution. Flag Day occurs on June 20, the day on which the designer of Argentina's flag, Manuel Belgrano, died. The Argentine motto is "In Union and Liberty."

states, each province has a capital and its own government. Like the federal government, the provincial governments are divided into three branches. A governor heads the executive branch in each province. Within the provinces are cities and towns, most of which are governed by mayors.

Mauricio Macri became mayor of Buenos Aires in 2007.

Buenos Aires: Capital City

The capital of Argentina and by far the largest city is Buenos Aires. According to the 2010 census, Buenos Aires was home to 2,890,151 people, but the metropolitan area is home to more than 13 million people, about one-third of the nation's entire population. People from Buenos Aires are sometimes called *porteños*, meaning "people of the port." This is because their ancestors arrived from Europe through the city's port.

Buenos Aires is Argentina's economic engine. It has the largest port in South America, dominates the nation's banking industry, and is a center for food processing, automobile manufacturing, and other industries.

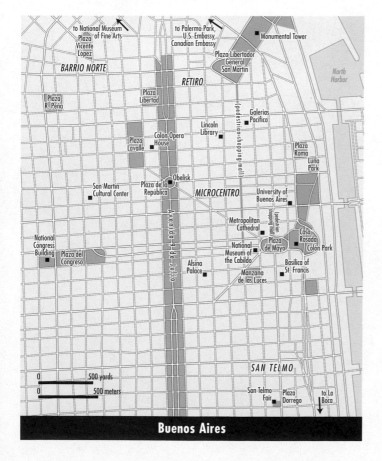

Buenos Aires

Buenos Aires is a grand city, where buildings constructed in a European style line broad streets. Avenida 9 de Julio (above), which runs through downtown Buenos Aires, is said to be the widest street in the world. The street is a full city block wide, and seven lanes of traffic flow in each direction. The street's name commemorates the date of Argentina's independence. Many monumental buildings line the street, including the Teatro Colón, one of the world's great opera houses. Sitting in the middle of the street is the Obelisk, a soaring monument as tall as a twenty-two-story building. It was built in 1936 to celebrate the city's four-hundredth birthday. Sports fans often gather at the Obelisk to celebrate victories.

Buenos Aires also has many other fascinating neighborhoods. La Boca is a brightly painted neighborhood where many artists work. Recoleta is an old quarter with beautiful stores and fancy hotels. The National Museum of Fine Arts and many other museums and university buildings are located there. It is said that the dance called the tango first gained recognition in the clubs of the Recoleta.

Downtown Buenos Aires is traversed by colorful buses. A subway system, called *el subte* (short for "subterranean"), runs beneath the city. One of the oldest in the world, it was started in 1912 and is decorated with tile murals.

CHAPTER 6

Making a Living

IN NORTHWESTERN ARGENTINA, AMONG BEAUTIFUL rocky mountains and tangled jungles, is a long valley called Quebrada de Humahuaca. This valley served as a trade route for indigenous peoples for at least ten thousand years. Today, Argentina is still one of the great trading nations of the world.

In the early twentieth century, Argentina had one of the eighth-largest economies in the world. But decades of political instability doomed the nation's economic advances. In recent years, Argentina has again improved its economy. It now has one of the highest incomes per person in South America, and the unemployment rate—the percentage of people who cannot find work—was just over 7 percent in 2014.

Opposite: **An Argentine science teacher gives a lecture. Teachers are part of the service sector of the economy.**

Agriculture

Argentina has almost 70 million acres (28 million hectares) of permanent cropland, making it one of the greatest food-producing countries in the world. Citrus fruits, cotton, and sugarcane are grown in some northern regions. But most of the agricultural land is in the Pampas. The crops that grow on the range include soybeans, corn, and wheat.

Soybeans are among Argentina's main exports. Most of the soybeans are sold to China. Although Argentines have limited the amount of land that can be owned by foreigners, China has contracted with some provincial governments

Argentina is the third-largest soybean producer in the world. Only the United States and Brazil produce more soybeans.

to lease land for agriculture to ensure China's food supply. Soybean crops have become so important in the southern part of Argentina that the region is sometimes called the United Republic of Soybeans.

Argentina is the world's fifth-largest wine producer. Much of it is malbec, a red wine that has grown in popularity the world over. Many of Argentina's malbec grapes are grown in the foothills of the Andes in Mendoza Province, in the west-central part of the country.

Cattle once roamed on Argentina's vast plains that are now planted with crops. Today, a large percentage of Argentine cattle are grown in feedlots, where they are penned in and fed for quick growth. This way of producing beef has marked the end of an era. Gauchos, the cowboys who watched over the cattle on the Pampas, have become a thing of the past.

A man harvests grapes in Mendoza, the heart of Argentina's wine industry.

What Argentina Grows, Makes, and Mines

AGRICULTURE (2011)

Soybeans	48,878,771 metric tons
Sugarcane	25,000,000 metric tons
Cattle	54,000,000 head

MANUFACTURING

Motor vehicles (2013)	791,007 units
Food processing (value of exports, 2007)	US$7,800,000,000
Steel (2013)	5,200,000 metric tons

MINING

Oil (2013)	796,300 barrels per day
Coal (2009)	228,782,000 metric tons
Copper (2011)	116,968 metric tons

Sheep ranches are plentiful in Patagonia. The largest owner of sheep is Benetton, a European clothing manufacturer. In the 1990s, Benetton bought more than 2 million acres (900,000 ha) of land in Patagonia. The Mapuche people, who traditionally lived in the area, have not been treated well. They have been pushed to the edges of their land, where they find it hard to make a living.

Cattle and sheep cannot thrive at the higher altitudes, but the domesticated camel relatives called llamas and alpacas can. The Quechua people of the Andes breed these animals for their wool, their milk, and their ability to carry heavy loads through the mountains.

Manufacturing

In recent years, the government has worked to encourage manufacturing and exports. Between 2003 and 2007, Argentina's industrial exports grew at 19 percent per year. Wages have increased as well.

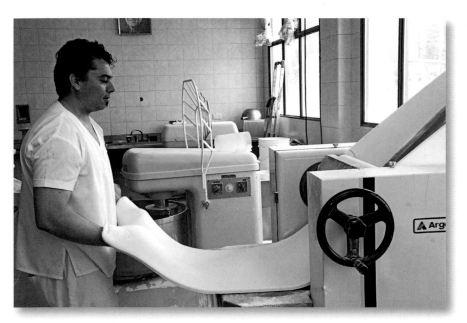

A baker in Tierra del Fuego uses a machine to roll out dough.

Argentina's primary industry has long been the manufacturing of food products. This industry employs about 30 percent of the workers in the nation. Other sectors are now growing, especially communications equipment and motor vehicles.

The center of Argentina's industrial production is the city of Córdoba. The biggest employers there are automobile manufacturers. They make cars for American and European car companies, including Peugeot and General Motors. Taxes are high on cars imported into Argentina, encouraging people to buy the cars manufactured in their own country.

Services

About seven out of every ten workers in Argentina work in service industries. In service industries, people do something for others, rather than making or growing products. These include industries such as health care, banking, sales, education, and transportation. Tourism has become a large part of the service sector, employing people in hotels, restaurants, ski resorts, and shops. Nearly six million foreign visitors traveled to Argentina in 2012.

Gold and More

It was gold that brought the Spaniards to South America more than four hundred years ago, and gold is still bringing outsiders to Argentina. The nation's largest open-pit mine, called La Alumbrera, is owned and run in part by a Canadian company. Located in the northwest, it produces both gold and copper.

More than half the world's supply of lithium ore comes from mines on the border between Argentina and Chile. Lithium is used in manufacturing ceramics, metal alloys, and batteries. In this region, tin, lead, zinc, and uranium are also mined.

Energy

Most of Argentina's electricity is supplied by natural gas and hydropower (running water). Most of the rivers used for

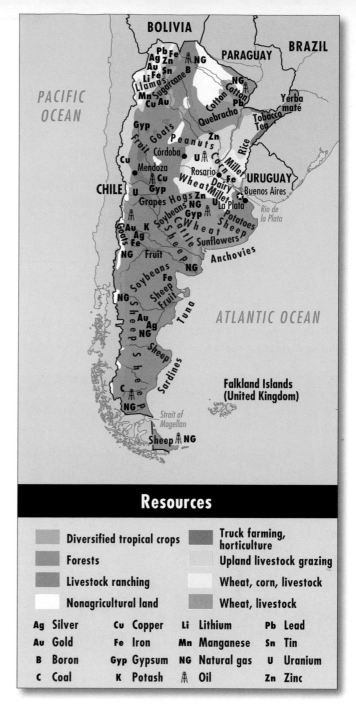

Resources

Diversified tropical crops	Truck farming, horticulture
Forests	Upland livestock grazing
Livestock ranching	Wheat, corn, livestock
Nonagricultural land	Wheat, livestock

Ag	Silver	Cu	Copper	Li	Lithium	Pb	Lead
Au	Gold	Fe	Iron	Mn	Manganese	Sn	Tin
B	Boron	Gyp	Gypsum	NG	Natural gas	U	Uranium
C	Coal	K	Potash	⚒	Oil	Zn	Zinc

electric power are located on the eastern side of the country. There are only two nuclear power plants in the country.

The winds blow hard across the open lands of Patagonia, so the government is expecting wind power to become increasingly important in coming years. On the Pampas, where there are few trees, the use of solar power will also increase. Right now, however, it is used only in very remote areas.

In 2010, Argentina was found to have huge shale-oil reserves in an area known as Vaca Muerta, meaning "dead cow." It is located in Neuquén Province, near the border with Chile. The oil is not in a large pool underground. Instead, it is

Oil rig workers drill wells in the Argentine desert.

part of the rock. To extract the oil, the shale must be crushed and heated to high temperatures. Natural gas is also found in the shale. To get the gas, the shale is broken using a process called hydraulic fracturing, more commonly known as hydro-fracking or fracking.

President Kirchner has made a deal with Chevron, an American oil company, to extract the oil. Chevron, hoping that Argentina's economy stabilizes, is investing huge amounts of money in recovering the oil. Chevron is working in partnership with the national Argentine oil company called YPF.

Thousands of Argentines, especially Mapuche Indians, have protested the development of fracking in the shale-oil fields. They fear it will cause serious water pollution and damage to the land.

People protest the Argentine government's agreement to allow Chevron and YFP to recover oil through fracking in Patagonia. Argentina is believed to have the world's fourth-largest reserves of shale oil.

CHAPTER 7

People and Language

I N 2014, ARGENTINA HAD AN ESTIMATED POPULATION of just over forty-three million. Because of its great open spaces and its relatively few people, it has a population density of just 38 people per square mile (15 per sq km), which is quite low. The United States, for example, has a population density of 84 people per square mile (32 per sq km), even though it also has a lot of wide-open spaces.

City and Country

In 2013, 92.8 percent of the Argentine population lived in cities. Only 7.2 percent lived in rural areas. This makes Argentina one of the most urbanized nations in the world.

Most people in big cities such as Buenos Aires live in tall apartment buildings. Outside of the city center, many people live in small houses made of concrete. In some slums and rural areas, people live in shacks, without access to drinking water.

Population of Major Cities (2010 est.)	
Buenos Aires	2,890,151
Córdoba	1,329,604
Rosario	1,193,605
Mendoza	957,000
La Plata	654,324

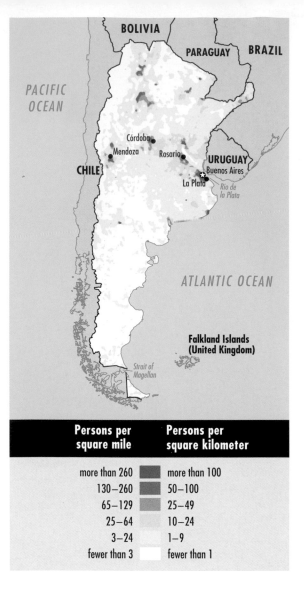

Persons per square mile		Persons per square kilometer
more than 260		more than 100
130–260		50–100
65–129		25–49
25–64		10–24
3–24		1–9
fewer than 3		fewer than 1

Indigenous Peoples

The Inca people ruled an empire in South America in the 1400s and early 1500s. It was headquartered in Peru, at Cusco, but it stretched into northwest Argentina. The main language of the empire was Quechua. Most of the Incas died from disease and warfare after the Spanish arrived, but the Quechua language is still spoken by many Argentines. Some English words come from the Quechua, including *condor*, *llama*, and *gaucho*.

The Diaguita people were farmers in the northwest. They were split up into many separate groups, most of which were conquered by the Incas. Today, only about thirty thousand Diaguita people remain.

The Mapuche people live in lands farther south, especially in Patagonia. Their name means "people of the land." Because European settlers were not much interested

A Helping Hand

Argentina is working to improve the lot of the poor. In 2009, the nation started a universal child allowance, which gives cash to low-income families with children. That single move lifted many Argentines out of poverty. Another policy that had a dramatic effect on poverty was the expansion of old-age pensions. All elderly Argentines now have guaranteed pensions.

in their lands at first, the Mapuches were largely left alone until the late 1800s. During the Conquest of the Desert from 1860 to 1885, many Mapuches were killed. Today, there are probably about one hundred thousand Mapuche people in Argentina, making them the largest indigenous group in the country. Many more Mapuches live in neighboring Chile.

After the fall of the military regime in 1983, some indigenous peoples began to claim the lands they had once occupied. In 1985, President Raúl Alfonsín signed a law granting full citizenship rights to native people in Argentina,

Mapuche people live throughout Argentina, but the largest numbers are in northern Patagonia.

The Wichí people of northern Argentina have lost much of their traditional land to soybean farmers.

but they sometimes have a difficult time holding on to their land, which is attractive to outside investors.

Changing Populations

During the colonial period, many enslaved Africans were brought into the country. By the mid-1800s, they made up about 15 percent of the population. Today, the black and mixed-race people make up only about 1 percent of the Argentine population.

Indigenous Peoples and the 1994 Constitution

In 1994, the Law of Indigenous Rights was added to the Argentine Constitution. For the first time in Argentine history, the government acknowledged the rights of indigenous peoples. Another change to the constitution was the removal of the old goal of promoting the conversion of Indians to Catholicism.

In the mid-1800s, Argentina started a movement to bring Europeans to the country. And they came, in large numbers, from Italy, Spain, Poland, Russia, Germany, Ireland, and France. Immigrants from Japan also arrived. This influx of people from all over the world overwhelmed the population of indigenous people and people of African descent.

Like the United States, Argentina can be called a melting pot because people from many different parts of the world came together to form a new nation. Argentina is second only to the United States in admitting the most immigrants. Perhaps 6.6 million people immigrated to Argentina from Europe between 1857 and 1950. Today, about 97 percent of Argentines have European ancestry, the highest percentage of any Latin American country. By contrast, less than 50 percent of Brazilians have European ancestry.

Buildings in the town of La Cumbrecita, in central Argentina, reflect the German origins of the people who first settled it.

Ethnic Argentina

White	97%
Indigenous, black, and other	3%

Lebanese immigrants perform during an event celebrating immigrants in Argentina.

Italians accounted for about half the immigration wave to Argentina in the nineteenth and early twentieth centuries. Today, more than half the people in Argentina have Italian ancestry, and many people in Buenos Aires speak Italian.

Unlike in other Latin American countries, most Europeans in Argentina did not have children with native people. Today, *mestizos*, people of mixed European and indigenous ancestry, make up only 14 percent of the population. In neighboring Chile, mestizos make up about 60 percent of the population.

Day of Respect

In many countries in Central and South America, Columbus Day, October 12, is called *Día de la Raza*, or the Day of the Race. It celebrates the arrival of Columbus in the Americas and the creation of Hispanic culture. The holiday has been observed in Argentina since 1917, but many people object to celebrating an event that led to the destruction of indigenous civilizations. Since 2010, Argentina has instead celebrated the second Monday in October as the Day of Respect for Cultural Diversity.

More Recent Immigrants

In the late twentieth century, immigration to Argentina once again increased. This time, many people came from eastern Europe and Arab lands, particularly what are now Lebanon and Syria. Many people also arrived from China, South Korea, and other Asian nations.

People from neighboring countries have also moved into Argentina. They came because Argentina's economy was in better shape than the economies of their home countries. There are more Paraguayans in Buenos Aires, for example, than there are in Asunción, the capital of Paraguay.

Argentine Spanish

Spanish is the official language of Argentina, but there are some differences between Argentine Spanish and that used in other Latin American countries. To start with, Argentines do

A Chinese man sells snacks during a Chinese New Year celebration. About 120,000 Argentines are of Chinese descent.

In addition to Spanish, which is the official language of Argentina, Guaraní, the language of many different native groups, is also an official language in the northeastern province of Corrientes. Guaraní words that have entered the English language include *jaguar* and *tapioca*.

not call their language Spanish. They call it *castellano*, meaning Castilian, from the Castile region of Spain. In Buenos Aires, the street slang used by the lower classes is called *lunfardo*. It grew out of words used by immigrants from different parts of the world to communicate with one another. Many of the words are based on Italian because Italian immigrants were so numerous.

One of the most common changes to Spanish in Argentina is the use of *vos* for *tú*, meaning "you," when speaking to someone who is a close friend or relative. Sometimes the verb following *vos* is pronounced differently, with a different emphasis than regular Spanish. For example, "you eat" is usu-

Some schools near Guaraní villages in northern Argentina are bilingual. In addition to Spanish, the children learn the Guaraní language and about Guaraní culture and music.

ally pronounced *vos comes* (vos koh-mess), with no emphasis on any syllable. But in Argentina, it is usually *vos comes* (vos koh-MESS), with the emphasis on the last syllable.

There are other words that Argentines use instead of standard Spanish. Rather than saying "*bueno*" for "great" or "good," they say "*joya.*" "Gasoline" is *nafta* instead of *gasolina*. Argentines tend to call almost anyone—a friend, a taxi driver, a waiter—*che*, meaning something like "buddy" or "pal."

In Spanish, a speaker uses a different form of a verb when talking to friends than when talking to strangers.

Common Terms in Argentine Spanish

Buenos días	Good morning
Hola	Hello
Por favor	Please
Gracias	Thank you
Chau or Adiós	Good-bye
¿Habla usted inglés?	Do you speak English?

CHAPTER 8

Spiritual Life

IN JUJUY PROVINCE IN NORTHWESTERN ARGENTINA, some Quechua people honor an earth goddess called Pachamama. She is one of a family of gods said to control life, harvests, and the universe. According to Incan tradition, this family of gods was headed by Inti, the sun god. Beliefs such as these are common in that part of Argentina.

The Mapuche people of the south believe in communicating with spirits through a shaman, who is usually a wise woman. These spirits fall into three main categories—ancestral spirits, nature spirits, and evil spirits. The Mapuche believe that these spirits play a role in the lives of individuals.

Opposite: **A statue of Pachamama. In the Andes today, some people perform rituals honoring Pachamama with offerings of food.**

The Coming of Christianity

When the Spanish arrived in the Americas carrying weapons and their faith in the Roman Catholic Church, they tried to wipe out the non-Christian beliefs of the people who

Sun of May

An important symbol in Argentina is called Sun of May. It is a sun figure with a face and thirty-two rays, and represents the Quechua sun god Inti. The Sun of May was depicted on the first Argentine coin, in 1813. Today, it appears on the Argentine flag.

lived there. Over time, Argentina became a predominantly Catholic country. Today's constitution gives Argentines freedom to worship as they wish. But in fact, religion is not central to the identity of most Argentines. In Buenos Aires, in particular, people live a more secular, or nonreligious, life than most Latin Americans.

The Children of Llullaillaco

In 1999, the frozen bodies of three Inca children were found on the summit of a 22,000-foot (6,700 m) volcano called Mount Llullaillaco, along the border between Argentina and Chile. The children had apparently been sacrificed about five hundred years ago in an Incan religious practice called *capacocha*. The children froze to death at such a great altitude that their bodies never thawed, and they became some of the best-preserved mummies ever found. The mummies were not shown in public until 2007, when the oldest of the three children, a fifteen-year-old girl nicknamed *La Doncella*, meaning "The Maiden," was displayed at the Museum of High Altitude Archaeology in Salta, which was once part of the Inca Empire. The mummies of the children are displayed in a special case that keeps them at freezing temperatures.

That does not mean that the Catholic Church—and its headquarters in Rome, Italy—does not play an important role in Argentine life. That role has changed frequently over the years, often depending on the attitude of the nation's president. In Argentina, the church and politics are usually intertwined. Sometimes they work together and sometimes they oppose each other. During the dark period of the Dirty War, some people suspected that many priests worked with the military. Not until the twenty-first century did leaders of the Catholic Church in Argentina apologize for its role in the Dirty War.

The head of the Roman Catholic Church is the pope, who works from the church headquarters in Vatican City, located within the city of Rome, Italy. The pope is elected by leading priests called cardinals. Argentina has four cardinals. One of them, Jorge Bergoglio, a native of Buenos Aires and of Italian

Argentines at a Mass in Buenos Aires. About a quarter of Argentines attend church regularly.

The Argentine Pope

Jorge Bergoglio was born in Buenos Aires in 1936. His father had immigrated from Italy in 1929 and married an Argentine of Italian descent. Jorge trained to be a chemist but after a serious illness he changed his focus and became a priest in 1969. Bergoglio served in several different countries and became adept at several languages. In 1992, he was named bishop of Buenos Aires and began his climb up the ranks of the Catholic leadership, but he never forgot his main concern: the poor.

He himself lived a humble life. Instead of living in a bishop's palace, he lived in a small apartment and took public transportation to get around (below, right). He washed the feet of criminals and the homeless at Easter, something that Jesus is said to have done.

On February 28, 2013, Pope Benedict XVI announced that he would resign from his position. Thirteen days later, the cardinals of the church voted to make the humble Argentine priest the new pope. Bergoglio took the name Francis, after St. Francis of Assisi, a thirteenth-century priest who helped the poor and became patron saint of animals and the environment.

Pope Francis has kept up his habit of living simply. After moving to Rome, he shunned the fancy apartments used by previous popes. Most of the gifts people around the world give him are auctioned off, and the Vatican uses the money to help the poor. His humility and his openness to people of all faiths—or of no faith— have made the Argentine pope popular the world over.

descent, was himself elected pope in 2013. He is the first pope to come from either North or South America.

Roman Catholicism remains a more important part of life for many Argentines outside of Buenos Aires. Many small towns and villages hold religious festivals that feature parades of Catholic statues through the streets. One special ritual honors a woman named Deolinda Correa. She was the wife of a soldier in the 1840 civil war. She died of starvation and

The Cathedral of La Plata is one of the largest churches in the Americas.

Religion in Argentina	
Roman Catholic	92%
Protestant	2%
Jewish	2%
Other	4%

thirst in an arid region of western Argentina. Soldiers found her body lying by the side of the road. Legend has it that her baby was still nursing at her breast, even though she had been dead for several days. The soldiers called it a miracle and built a shrine where she was buried. Many Argentines make pilgrimages to her shrine to pray for miracles. Officially, the church disapproves of such actions.

A similar legend is that of Gauchito Gil. He was an army deserter who became an outlaw known for taking money from

Pilgrims place offerings near a statue of Deolinda Correa in Vallecito in western Argentina.

the rich and giving it to the poor people who protected him from the authorities. He was finally captured in 1878. When a policeman began torturing him, Gil said that the man's son was very ill, and that the only way the officer could save the

About one hundred thousand people visit the main shrine to Gauchito Gil every January 8, the anniversary of his death.

The Statue in the Mountains

In 1902, Argentina and Chile came very close to going to war over the border between the two countries. The people urged their governments to settle the dispute without war. The government asked the U.S. ambassador and the British king to decide on the border. Argentina and Chile accepted their decision peacefully. To commemorate the occasion, a huge statue of Jesus, called *Christ Redeemer of the Andes*, sculpted by Argentine artist Mateo Alonso, stands at 13,000 feet (4,000 m) on the border facing Mount Aconcagua.

Spiritual Life **99**

People chat after a Mormon church service in Buenos Aires.

boy was to pray to him, Gauchito Gil. The policeman slit Gil's throat anyway. When the officer returned home, he found that his son was indeed ill, so he prayed to the man he had just killed, and the son recovered. Shrines to Gauchito Gil are now located throughout the country.

Other Christians

A small percentage of Argentines belong to Christian churches other than the Roman Catholic Church. Most non-Catholics are members of the Church of Jesus Christ of Latter-day Saints, or Mormons. Almost four hundred thousand Mormons throughout Argentina belong to eight hundred different congregations.

Another major group of non-Catholics are evangelicals. They take the Bible as their source for all beliefs and behaviors.

Other Religions

Argentina is home to about 230,000 Jewish people, more than any other nation in Central or South America. Buenos Aires has more than twenty synagogues, or Jewish houses of worship. Cities such as Córdoba, Rosario, and Tucumán also have synagogues.

Argentina also has the largest Muslim population in Latin America. It is estimated at more than four hundred thousand. Most Argentine Muslims are of Arab descent. The largest mosque, or Islamic house of worship, in Latin America is King Fahd Islamic Cultural Center in Buenos Aires. Carlos Menem, who was president from 1989 to 1999, is an Arab whose parents were from Syria.

The King Fahd Islamic Cultural Center includes a mosque and several schools.

CHAPTER 9

Athletes and Artists

ARGENTINA COMES TO A HALT DURING IMPORTANT soccer matches. Streets clear out except around store windows where a TV is showing the match. From young children to older adults, everyone watches and cares about the outcome.

Soccer, which Argentines call football, was brought to Argentina by British sailors more than 150 years ago. By 1887, Argentines were playing it professionally and it was called association football. Today, both professional and amateur soccer make up the biggest sport in the country, and throughout South America. Young children learn to play in the streets. Older children play in clubs. And adults play in both amateur and professional clubs. And if they're not playing, they're watching and cheering. There are more than three thousand football clubs across the nation. They are an important part of life in Argentina. Almost all Argentines have allegiance to one association soccer team or another.

Opposite: **A boy plays soccer in Buenos Aires.**

Young Heroes

Sergio Agüero—called Kun, a name given him by his grandparents—was the youngest player to enter the Argentine First Division, the nation's top league. He was only fifteen at the time. Five years later, he led Argentina to a gold medal at the 2008 Olympics. Agüero began playing soccer in Europe in 2006 and soon became the highest goal scorer on the Manchester City team in England.

Lionel Messi (right) is one of Argentina's favorite soccer stars. He is captain of the Argentine national team but plays as a forward for Barcelona in Spain. Messi was born in Rosario, in central Argentina. At the age of eleven, he was diagnosed with a growth problem, but he showed enough promise in the sport that the Barcelona team was willing to pay his medical expenses. He grew, and Barcelona sent him through its youth training program. Messi began playing professionally in 2004, at age seventeen. In 2008, he led the Argentine national team to a gold medal in the Olympics. In the 2011–2012 season, he set the European record for the most goals scored in a single season, with seventy-three, including a record-breaking five goals in a single match. He is routinely the top scorer in Europe, and many people consider him the best player in the world.

Argentines take their soccer matches very seriously, and sometimes their passion turns violent. Most stadiums have high fences that prevent people in the stands from going onto the field. Because of the potential for violence, women and children seldom attend professional soccer games in Argentina. However, Argentine women do play soccer on an amateur basis. They now have a national team that plays in the Olympics and the Women's World Cup.

The soccer championship of South America is determined in a competition called Copa América (America Cup), which is held every four years. Argentina has won the Copa América fourteen times since it began in 1916, and has hosted the games more times than any other country.

Other Sports

Soccer is not the only sport that Argentines love. In the 1980s, many small local leagues joined together as the Liga Nacional de Básquet (National Basketball League). It consists of sixteen teams. Argentina's national basketball team won the 2004 Summer Olympics with forward Walter Herrmann as the key player. Herrmann also played professional basketball in the United States, with the Charlotte Bobcats and the Detroit Pistons of the National Basketball Association.

Rugby, a sport similar to American football but played without helmets and padding,

Walter Herrmann played in the National Basketball Association for three years.

is growing in popularity in Argentina. The national team is drawing more fans with its winning ways. By 2014, Argentina was ranked twelfth among rugby teams in the world.

Argentines also play the new sport called footgolf. It uses golf courses and the rules of golf, but the ball is kicked like a soccer ball. The Federation for International Footgolf held its first World Cup in 2012 in Budapest, Hungary, with Argentine players participating. Argentines came in fourth and fifth in the competition.

The sport of footgolf is growing quickly in Argentina. One of the world's top-ranked players, Christian Otero, is an Argentine.

The National Sport?

You might think that soccer would be Argentina's national sport because it is so popular, but that game is played everywhere around the world. Argentina's national sport is peculiarly Argentine. Called *pato*, which means "duck" in Spanish, it is a combination of basketball and polo. It was originally played by gauchos, who used a live duck in a basket instead of a ball. Today, players use a ball that has six handles wrapped around it, making it easy to grab. Teams of four riders compete for control of the ball, trying to throw it through a vertical hoop.

Polo, which shows off Argentina's great horses as well as their riders, is very popular. This team sport has four riders on horseback using long mallets to try to hit balls into the opposing team's goal. Argentina is one of the few countries where polo is played professionally. The Polo World Cup Championship has been held since 1987, and Argentina has won most of the events.

Argentina's snow-covered Andes Mountains draw skiers and snowboarders from all over the world. The prime season in Argentina is June to October. Many skiers from North America head to Patagonia when it is winter there, but summer in the Northern Hemisphere, so they can ski year-round. Las Leñas, in the central Andes near Mendoza, is an important ski area. The slopes are above the tree line and they get frequent fresh snow. Ski teams from many nations, including the United States, have practiced there.

The bandonion is a type of accordion that is essential to tango music.

Car racing is popular throughout Argentina. The oldest car race series in the world is Turismo Carretera, or TC competition. It has been run since 1937. The races have mostly pitted Ford cars against Chevrolets. Other races, using smaller cars, have been spun off from the TC.

Dancing to the Beat

Different regions of Argentina have their own style of music. Sometimes one rises to great popularity for a while, and then another rises. They have names such as *cordobesa* (from Córdoba) or *santafesina* (from Santa Fe).

Argentina is best known for its music and dance called the tango. Tango music tends to be somewhat slow and sad, and the dance very dramatic and expressive. It originated in the working class neighborhoods of Buenos Aires in the late nineteenth century. The tango was not accepted by the middle and upper classes of Argentina until it first became popular in Europe and then returned home. The tango has become popular again today. For eighteen days during August, a massive tango festival is held in and around Buenos Aires. Everyone is welcome to watch, enjoy, and participate in this romantic dance.

Although Argentina is best known for the tango, its national dance is the zamba. This is a dance performed by couples with majesty and elegance, often telling a story of Argentine history. The dancers move around each other, waving handkerchiefs. The zamba originated in Tucumán Province of northern Argentina almost two hundred years ago.

A couple demonstrates the tango in Buenos Aires. The tango is a slow dance, with many long pauses.

Argentine folksinger Mercedes Sosa introduced folk music with a social conscience in the 1960s, so she became known as the "voice of the voiceless ones." This Grammy-award winner was born in San Miguel de Tucumán. One of her grandfathers was a French immigrant, and another was a Quechua-speaking Indian. Sosa was much loved in Argentina, and when she died in 2009, the nation held three days of mourning for her.

The Cosquín Festival, held in Córdoba, is one of the most important folk music festivals in Latin America. Another major music festival held in Argentina is called Ultra Buenos Aires.

Many of Mercedes Sosa's songs commented on the political and social issues of the day. During the military dictatorship of the 1970s, she was forced to leave Argentina.

This two-day festival of electronic music features world-renowned DJs. Both of these events are held during the Argentine summer.

Argentina also has a long history of classical music. Pianists the world over perform music by Alberto Ginastera. Born in Buenos Aires, he often used Argentine folk themes, including those of the gauchos, in his compositions. He wrote operas and ballets, as well as orchestral music.

Telling Stories

Literature is a major art form in Argentina. Today, writers are highly valued there, but that hasn't always been the case. During the Dirty War of the 1970s, many writers who disagreed with the government went into exile in other countries. In the years since, they have returned to celebrate their country.

Today, Argentina is very supportive of its writers. Buenos Aires has a huge number of bookstores, which often stay open far into the night. In 2012, Buenos Aires voted to provide pensions to the writers who live there if they are over sixty years old and have written at least five books. That plan may go nationwide.

Alberto Ginastera, one of the most important Latin American composers, also taught composition at several music schools.

Jorge Luis Borges stands on the terrace outside his home in Buenos Aires. Borges is considered one of the world's greatest writers of the twentieth century.

Jorge Luis Borges wrote many stories and poems involving Buenos Aires. He called his native Buenos Aires a city "I judge to be as eternal as water and air." He first made his name as the editor of a literary magazine called *Martín Fierro* after the gaucho hero of an epic poem written in the 1870s by José Hernández. Borges became known for his short stories that merge philosophy and dark, dreamlike fantasy. By the time he died in 1986, Borges was celebrated throughout the world.

María Elena Walsh was a poet and musician best known for her songs and stories for children, especially those featuring a little turtle named Manuelita and a silly monkey named Mono Liso. Music and movies made from her stories are still popular.

Argentina is a center for the production of *telenovelas*, serial TV dramas similar to soap operas that usually last for a few months. Many shows are intended for children and

teenagers. Popular shows include *Guapas*, which means "handsome" or "gorgeous," and *Violetta*, about a musical teenager. Argentine telenovelas are often shown on the Latin America Disney Channel.

Martina Stoessel, the star of *Violetta*, performs in concert as her character.

Nobel Prizes

Two Argentines have been awarded the Nobel Peace Prize. In 1936, this honor went to Carlos Saavedra Lamas (1878–1959). As president of the League of Nations (a forerunner of the United Nations), he helped settle a conflict between Paraguay and Bolivia. In 1980, Adolfo Pérez Esquivel (1931–), shown here, was honored for his work in human rights in Argentina. Though he trained as a sculptor and architect, he gave that up to work with nonviolent organizations in Latin America. He helped persuade the United Nations to establish its Human Rights Commission.

Three Argentina-born scientists have won Nobel Prizes. First was Bernardo Houssay in 1947 for physiology or medicine. Luis Federico Leloir won in 1970 for chemistry, and César Milstein won in 1984, also for physiology or medicine.

CHAPTER 10

School, Food, and Families

EDUCATION HAS LONG BEEN IMPORTANT IN Argentina. Literacy is high. About 98 percent of people over the age of ten can read and write. This is one of the highest literacy rates in the world. Education is free to all Argentines, even at the university level.

Opposite: **Children leave school in Buenos Aires.**

School Time

Since 2011, all Argentine children have been required to attend school for twelve years. In Buenos Aires, primary education lasts to grade six. Secondary school, or high school, lasts another six years. Beyond the big city, primary school continues through grade seven. Students study subjects such as math, science, history, and Spanish. In addition, every child studies English in school. Most Argentine children wear uniforms to school. This is meant to show equality among all students.

Some young people in Argentina also take classes outside of school. This girl is enrolled in a video course.

The school day in Argentina is shorter than it is in the United States, lasting only four or five hours. The school year lasts from March to December.

In the distant parts of the country, where most of the indigenous people live, education is not so readily available. The children there are often given scholarships to attend

The Tooth Mouse

In Argentina, children don't talk about the tooth fairy. Instead, they talk about a little mouse that takes their lost tooth from under the pillow and leaves some coins. The mouse is named El Rátón Pérez, or Pérez the Mouse, a character popularized by Spanish writer Luis Coloma in a story he wrote in 1894 for Alfonso XIII, an eight-year-old boy who was the king of Spain. Today, the character is popular in many Spanish-speaking countries.

distant high schools, but that takes them away from their families. Also, because all schools in the country use the same European-oriented curriculum, they often find little of value in it that applies to their own lives.

About half of the young people in Argentina attend college. In addition, thousands of college students from all over Latin America study in Argentina. The nation's top-ranked university, and the largest in Latin America, is the University of Buenos Aires. Its buildings are spread throughout the city.

The University of Buenos Aires is the largest school in Latin America, enrolling about three hundred thousand students.

A family enjoys a meal at a café in Buenos Aires.

The oldest university in the country is the National University of Córdoba. It was founded in 1613. Almost every other large city also has a national university.

Favorite Foods

Argentina has declared three food items to be national symbols. The first is *asado*, or barbeque. The second is *locro*, stew. And the third is *maté* (mah-TAY), a drink called the "national infusion," because, like coffee, its flavor comes from soaking a plant material in hot water. Maté is made from the dried leaves of the yerba maté plant, a barrel-shaped gourd. The leaves are placed into the maté cup, and hot water is poured into it. After it has steeped awhile, the tea is drunk through a metal straw with a spoon-shaped filter at the end. It's said that

Where's the Beef?

An *asado* is a gathering where people talk, laugh, and grill their own steaks on a communal grill. The meat, too, is called *asado*. But these barbeques are not as popular as they once were. For decades, Argentines ate more beef per person than people from any other country—more than twice as much as Americans. But in recent years, Argentines, like many people around the world, have been decreasing the amount of beef they eat. In 2013, they lost their status as the world's biggest consumer of beef to neighboring Uruguay.

Argentines use 200,000 tons of yerba maté leaves each year. The drink is now popular in many parts of the world.

Yerba maté cup and leaves

A Hearty Locro

The name *locro* comes from the Quechua word *ruqru*. Every Latin American country has its own version of this dish, but the central ingredients are corn, potatoes, and some type of meat. This tasty meal, popularized by the gauchos, is often eaten in winter and is served at celebrations of the May Revolution. Have an adult help you with this recipe.

Ingredients

¼ cup olive oil

2 medium onions, chopped

2 cloves garlic, thinly sliced

2 pounds beef, cut into cubes

2 chorizos (spicy sausage), sliced

2 ears of fresh sweet corn, cut off the cob

1 teaspoon cumin

2 bay leaves

2 teaspoons paprika

1 can hominy (dried corn)

Hot water

1½ cups butternut squash, peeled and diced small

1½ cups yams, peeled and diced small

Salt and pepper to taste

Directions

Put the oil in a heavy pot and heat over medium heat. Add the onions, garlic, and meats and cook until the onions begin to look transparent. Add the fresh corn, cumin, bay leaves, and paprika and cook for ten minutes more. Add the hominy, including the liquid from the can. Add hot water to an inch or more above the ingredients. Stir in the squash and yams and bring to a boil. Turn down the heat to simmer, and cover the pot. Let the mixture cook for two hours, stirring every 15 minutes, smashing the softened ingredients against the side of the pot. The smashed vegetables will gradually thicken the stew. When the stew is done, season with salt and pepper. Serve and enjoy.

Medialunas are often coated with a sweet glaze. Argentines usually eat them with coffee.

The most common breakfast in Argentina is *medialunas*, which means "half-moons." These are sweet crescent-shaped rolls similar to croissants. Children sometimes drink a *submarino* for breakfast. This is a sugared hot milk with a chunk of chocolate (the "submarine") added. A favorite food of children and adults alike is *dulce de leche*, a sweet, gooey, caramel. It is often served between two cookies. Called *alfajores*, these treats can often be bought from vendors on the street. Other

foods bought from vendors include warm peanuts, empanadas (small meat-filled pies), popcorn, and fruit.

Buenos Aires has many closed-door restaurants. These are small restaurants, often in the chef's own home, where only a few

A chef prepares salads for diners who will be eating in his home.

Quinoa has been a staple food in the Andes for thousands of years. Its seeds are high in protein.

people can dine at a time. Diners only hear about these restaurants through word of mouth, and they must have a reservation.

Only recently has food of the indigenous peoples begun to play a part in restaurant meals in Argentina. The food of the Incas has become popular. This includes kebabs made of llama, alligator, and ñandu. Quinoa, a grain used by the Incas, is often served with the meats.

Late Nights

Visitors sometimes think that Argentines don't get any sleep. This is because dining out usually doesn't start until 10 o'clock at night, and the nightlife doesn't start until way after midnight. Argentines are able to handle this schedule because they generally take a nap before going out in the evening.

Throughout the country's history, most business and government offices closed for three or four hours in the middle of the day. People would go home to eat and take a nap during the hottest hours. The businesses would open again in the late afternoon, and people would work into the evening and have a late dinner. Because international business is more important now, Argentine businesses tend to be open during the daytime office hours that companies around the world usually share.

Keeping in Touch

Argentines are expert at keeping in touch with friends and family. In 2012, there were at least 150 cell phones for every 100 people in the country. Cell phone towers are also located

Most businesses in Argentina are now open throughout the day.

A priest in Argentina talks on a cell phone. The vast majority of adults in Argentina have cell phones.

throughout the country, even in deep Patagonia and distant Andes regions. However, some tourist places in the far south pride themselves on not having cell phone towers.

Argentines also love to talk in person. Conversation is considered an art to them. A favorite topic of conversation is government corruption. Discussing the latest scandals can occupy a group of friends for many long hours. People also while away the time discussing such things as how their favorite soccer teams are doing, who has the best doctors, and where the best beaches are found. Any subject is fair game.

One of the most popular holidays in Argentina is on July 20. It is not the anniversary of a battle, or the birthday of a prominent political hero. It is a phenomenon called Friend's

Day, an enduring part of the World Friendship Crusade that started in neighboring Paraguay in 1958 to promote peace. On this day, people get together after work, send one another greeting cards, and give gifts. Restaurants and cafés overflow with customers. Sometimes, Argentines make so many phone calls to friends on this day that the cell phone network fails because it is overwhelmed. It is a time when Argentines stop to acknowledge the people who make their lives better.

Argentine friends meet for a meal.

National Holidays

New Year's Day	January 1
Carnival and Shrove Tuesday	February or March
Memorial Day	March 24
Good Friday	March or April
Day of the Veterans	April 2
Labor Day	May 1
National Day	May 25
Flag Day	June 20
Independence Day	July 9
San Martín Day	August 17
Day of Respect for Cultural Diversity	Second Monday of October
National Sovereignty Day	November 24
Feast of the Immaculate Conception	December 8
Christmas	December 25

Timeline

ARGENTINE HISTORY

Ancient people paint the Cave of the Hands in Patagonia. **ca. 7300 BCE**

People begin farming in what is now Argentina. **ca. 5000 BCE**

WORLD HISTORY

ca. 2500 BCE The Egyptians build the pyramids and the Sphinx in Giza.

ca. 563 BCE The Buddha is born in India.

313 CE The Roman emperor Constantine legalizes Christianity.

610 The Prophet Muhammad begins preaching a new religion called Islam.

1054 The Eastern (Orthodox) and Western (Roman Catholic) Churches break apart.

1095 The Crusades begin.

1215 King John seals the Magna Carta.

1300s The Renaissance begins in Italy.

1347 The plague sweeps through Europe.

1453 Ottoman Turks capture Constantinople, conquering the Byzantine Empire.

1492 Columbus arrives in North America.

1500s Reformers break away from the Catholic Church, and Protestantism is born.

Spaniard Juan Díaz de Solís sails up the Río de la Plata. **1516 CE**

Ferdinand Magellan sails around Tierra del Fuego. **1520**

Pedro de Mendoza founds a fort at Buenos Aires. **1536**

Spaniards found Argentina's first permanent settlement, at Santiago del Estero. **1553**

Slave ships begin bringing enslaved Africans to Argentina. **Early 1700s**

ARGENTINE HISTORY

Spain creates the Viceroyalty of Río de la Plata, with Buenos Aires as its capital.	**1776**
Argentina declares itself self-ruling in the May Revolution.	**1810**
Argentina declares itself independent from Spain.	**1816**
Argentina's constitution is approved.	**1853**
Slavery is completely abolished in Argentina.	**1861**
The War of the Triple Alliance is fought.	**1865–1870**
Tierra del Fuego is split between Chile and Argentina.	**1881**
The military overthrows the president in a coup.	**1930**
Juan Perón becomes president.	**1946**
A military coup removes Perón from power. He goes into exile.	**1955**
The military again takes power; the Dirty War begins.	**1976**
Argentine troops invade the Falkland Islands; British troops force them out.	**1982**
Argentina returns to civilian control; Raúl Alfonsín is elected president.	**1983**
Argentina's economy crashes.	**2001**
Cristina Fernández de Kirchner becomes the first woman elected president of Argentina.	**2007**
Huge shale-oil reserves are discovered in Patagonia.	**2010**

WORLD HISTORY

1776	The U.S. Declaration of Independence is signed.
1789	The French Revolution begins.
1865	The American Civil War ends.
1879	The first practical lightbulb is invented.
1914	World War I begins.
1917	The Bolshevik Revolution brings communism to Russia.
1929	A worldwide economic depression begins.
1939	World War II begins.
1945	World War II ends.
1969	Humans land on the Moon.
1975	The Vietnam War ends.
1989	The Berlin Wall is torn down as communism crumbles in Eastern Europe.
1991	The Soviet Union breaks into separate states.
2001	Terrorists attack the World Trade Center in New York City and the Pentagon near Washington, D.C.
2004	A tsunami in the Indian Ocean destroys coastlines in Africa, India, and Southeast Asia.
2008	The United States elects its first African American president.

Fast Facts

Official name: Argentine Republic

Capital: Buenos Aires

Official language: Spanish

Buenos Aires

National flag

Andes Mountains

National anthem: "¡Oíd, Mortales!" ("Hear, O Mortals!")

Government: Federal republic

Head of state: President

Head of government: President

Area of country: 1,074,000 square miles (2,780,000 sq km)

Latitude and longitude of geographic center: 34°00' S, 64°00' W

Bordering countries: Uruguay to the east, Brazil to the northeast, Bolivia and Paraguay to the north, Chile to the west

Highest elevation: Mount Aconcagua, 22,834 feet (6,960 m) above sea level

Lowest elevation: Laguna del Carbón, 345 feet (105 m) below sea level

Average high temperatures:

	January	July
Northeastern Argentina	95°F (35°C)	73°F (23°C)
Buenos Aires	84°F (29°C)	57°F (14°C)
Southern Argentina	70°F (21°C)	43°F (6°C)

Average annual precipitation: 8 to 80 inches (20 to 200 cm)

Cave of the Hands

Currency

National population (2014 est.): 43,024,374

Population of major cities (2010 est.):

Buenos Aires	2,890,151
Córdoba	1,329,604
Rosario	1,193,605
Mendoza	957,000
La Plata	654,324

Landmarks:
- ▶ *Cave of the Hands*, Santa Cruz Province
- ▶ *Iguazú Falls*, Misiones Province
- ▶ *La Boca*, Buenos Aires
- ▶ *Perito Moreno Glacier*, Santa Cruz Province
- ▶ *Teatro Colón*, Buenos Aires

Economy: The service sector is the largest part of Argentina's economy. Banking, real estate, education, health care, and sales all play major roles. Tourism is growing in importance, and more people now travel to Argentina than to any other South American nation. Major industries in Argentina include food processing, car manufacturing, steel production, textile production, and oil refining. Argentina is a major producer of wheat, soybeans, beef, and wool.

Currency: The Argentine peso. In 2014, 1 peso equaled about US$0.12 and US$1.00 equaled 8.42 pesos.

System of weights and measures: Metric system

Literacy rate (2012): 98%

Schoolchildren

Jorge Luis Borges

Common Spanish words and phrases:

Buenos días	Good morning
Hola	Hello
Por favor	Please
Gracias	Thank you
¿Habla usted inglés?	Do you speak English?

Prominent Argentines:

Jorge Luis Borges (1899–1986)
Writer

Pope Francis (Jorge Bergoglio) (1936–)
Head of the Roman Catholic Church

Alberto Ginastera (1916–1983)
Classical music composer

Lionel Messi (1987–)
Soccer player

María Eva Duarte Perón (1919–1952)
First lady and political icon

Juan Domingo Perón (1895–1974)
President

José de San Martín (1778–1850)
Liberator of Argentina, Peru, and Chile

Mercedes Sosa (1935–2009)
Singer

To Find Out More

Books

▶ Dingus, Lowell, Luis M. Chiappe, and Rodolfo Coria. *Dinosaur Eggs Discovered! Unscrambling the Clues*. Minneapolis: Twenty-First Century Books, 2007.

▶ Gorrell, Gena K. *In the Land of the Jaguar: South America and Its People*. Toronto: Tundra Books, 2007.

▶ Stille, Darlene R. *Eva Perón: First Lady of Argentina*. Makato, MN: Compass Point Books, 2006.

Music

▶ Piazzolla, Astor. *Tango: Zero Hour*. New York: Nonesuch, 2007.

▶ *Rough Guide to the Music of Argentina*. London: World Music Network, 2004.

▶ Sosa, Mercedes. *30 Años*. Santa Monica, CA: PolyGram, 2005.

▶ Visit this Scholastic Web site for more information on Argentina:
www.factsfornow.scholastic.com
Enter the keyword **Argentina**

Index

Page numbers in *italics*
indicate illustrations.

Meet the Author

JEAN F. BLASHFIELD HAS WRITTEN MORE THAN 160 books, most of them for young people. Many of them have been for Scholastic's Enchantment of the World and America the Beautiful series. She has also created an encyclopedia of aviation and space, written popular books on murderers and houseplants (not in the same book), and had a lot of fun creating a book on the things women have done called *Hellraisers, Heroines, and Holy Women.* In addition, Blashfield founded the Dungeons & Dragons fantasy book department, which is now part of Wizards of the Coast.

Born in Madison, Wisconsin, Jean Blashfield grew up in the Chicago area. She graduated from the University of Michigan and worked for publishers in Chicago, New York, and London, and for NASA in Washington, D.C. She returned to Wisconsin when she married Wallace Black (a publisher, writer, and pilot) and began to raise a family. She has two grown children and three grandchildren.

Photo Credits

Photographs ©:

cover: Yadid Levy/Media Bakery; back cover: Martin Harvey/Getty Images; 2: Domingo Leiva/Getty Images; 5: Javier Larrea/age fotostock; 6 left: Russell Gordon/Zuma Press/Newscom; 6 center: Art Wolfe Stock/age fotostock; 6 right: David Gray/Reuters/Corbis Images; 7 left: James Kay/Danita Delimont Photography/Newscom; 7 right: Julian Finney/Getty Images; 8: Gareth Mccormack/Getty Images; 11: Jason Rothe/Alamy Images; 12: Tim Moore/Alamy Images; 13: Art Wolfe Stock/age fotostock; 14: National Geographic Image Collection/Alamy Images; 17: Raga/Iberfoto/The Image Works; 18: jozef sedmak/Thinkstock; 19 top: age fotostock/Superstock, Inc.; 19 bottom: James Kay/Danita Delimont Photography/Newscom; 20: Etcheverry Collection/Alamy Images; 21: Diego Giudice/KRT/Newscom; 22 top: JTB Media Creation, Inc./Alamy Images; 22 bottom: De Visu/Shutterstock, Inc.; 23: Y. Levy/Alamy Images; 24: Jason Edwards/Getty Images; 25: Chris Gomersall/Alamy Images; 26: HagePhoto/Getty Images; 27 left: Emiliano Rodriguez/Alamy Images; 27 right: Alexandre Fagundes De Fagundes/Dreamstime; 28: Ralf Hettler/Getty Images; 30 top: Juniors/Superstock, Inc.; 30 bottom: Wayne Lynch/age fotostock; 31: Lucidio Studio, Inc. Stock Connection Worldwide/Newscom; 32: lrh847/iStockphoto; 33 top: Diego Ivo Piacenza/age fotostock; 33 bottom: Joe McDonald/Corbis Images; 34: Angel Manzano/age fotostock/Superstock, Inc.; 35: age fotostock/Superstock, Inc.; 36: Nacho Calonge/Alamy Images; 37 top: Ingram Publishing/Newscom; 37 bottom: Wildlife GmbH/Alamy Images; 38: Hemis/Alamy Images; 39 top: Natacha Pisarenko/AP Images; 39 bottom: Reuters/Corbis Images; 40: Thom Lang/Alamy Images; 42: Hulton-Deutsch Collection/Corbis Images; 45: DEA/G. Dagli Orti/Getty Images; 47: DEA/G. Dagli Orti/Getty Images; 48 left: UniversalImagesGroup/Getty Images; 48 right: Universal History Archive/Getty Images; 49: DEA/G. Dagli Orti/Getty Images; 50: Oronoz/Album/Superstock, Inc.; 51: DeAgostini/Superstock, Inc.; 52: Everett Collection/Everett Collection; 53: National Geographic Stock, Vintage Coll./The Granger Collection; 54: Bettmann/Corbis Images; 55: Rue des Archives/The Granger Collection; 56 top: Keystone Pictures USA/Alamy Images; 56 bottom: Bettmann/Corbis Images; 57: Keystone/Getty Images; 58: Leo La Valle/EPA/Newscom; 59: Bettmann/Corbis Images; 60: Daniel Garcia/Getty Images; 61: Notimex/Newscom; 62: Anibal Trejo/Shutterstock, Inc.; 64: Juan Mabromata/Getty Images; 65 top: Victor R. Caivano/AP Images; 65 bottom: Leo La Valle/EFE/Newscom; 66: Victor R. Caivano/AP Images; 68: David Gray/Reuters/Corbis Images; 69: Ricardo Ceppi/picture-alliance/dpa/Newscom; 70 top: esancai/iStockphoto; 70 bottom: epa european pressphoto agency b.v./Alamy Images; 71: Chad Ehlers/Alamy Images; 72: GoGo Images Corporation/Alamy Images; 74: JMichl/iStockphoto; 75: Russell Gordon/Zuma Press/Newscom; 77 top: amybbb/Shutterstock, Inc.; 77 bottom: David Frazier/The Image Works; 78: Bloomberg/Getty Images; 80: Russell Gordon/Zuma Press/Newscom; 81: Daniel Jayo/EPA/Newscom; 82: David Frazier/The Image Works; 84: Jeffrey Greenberg/The Image Works; 85: Darius Panahpour/Danita Delimont; 86 top: Sergio Goya/dpa/Corbis Images; 86 bottom: Florian Kopp/imagebro/imageBroker/Superstock, Inc.; 87: C2070 Rolf Haid/dpa/Corbis Images; 88: Martin Zabala/Xinhua Press/Corbis Images; 89: Pablo Molina Xinhua News Agency/Newscom; 90: Jason Rothe/Alamy Images; 91: imageBroker/Alamy Images; 92: Getty Images; 94 top: DEA/G. Dagli Orti/Getty Images; 94 bottom: Natacha Pisarenko/AP Images; 95: Maxi Failla/Getty Images; 96 left: Emiliano Lasalvia/Getty Images; 96 right: Franco Origlia/Getty Images; 97: Evgeniya Uvarova/Dreamstime; 98: Therin-Weise/picture alliance/Arco Images G/Newscom; 99 top: Nacho Calonge/Alamy Images; 99 bottom: Florian Kopp imageBroker/Newscom; 100: Marcos Brindicci/Corbis Images; 101: Wide Eye Pictures/Alamy Images; 102: Julian Finney/Getty Images; 104: Franco Origlia/Getty Images; 105: Jeff Kowalsky/EPA/Newscom; 106: Xinhua/Alamy Images; 107: LatinContent/Getty Images; 108: David R. Frazier/Science Source; 109: Grafissimo/iStockphoto; 110: ERRG Photography/Alamy Images; 111: Leonard McCombe/Getty Images; 112: Mondadori/Getty Images; 113 top: Natacha Pisarenko/AP Images; 113 bottom: Alfredo Aldai/EPA/Newscom; 114: Image Source Plus/Alamy Images; 116 top: Florian Kopp/imagebro/imageBroker/Superstock, Inc.; 116 bottom: Paco Gómez García/Alamy Images; 117: Danita Delimont/Alamy Images; 118: David R. Frazier/The Image Works; 119 top: Jeremy Hoare/age fotostock; 119 bottom: Ferumov/Shutterstock, Inc.; 120: Tim Whitby/Alamy Images; 121: Michele Molinari/Alamy Images; 122 top: Stefano Paterna/Alamy Images; 122 bottom: Natacha Pisarenko/AP Images; 123: Tashka2000/Dreamstime; 124, 125: GoGo Images Corporation/Alamy Images; 126: David R. Frazier Photolibrary, Inc./Alamy Images; 127: Xinhua/Alamy Images; 130: Chad Ehlers/Alamy Images; 131 top: esancai/iStockphoto; 131 bottom: age fotostock/Superstock, Inc.; 132 top: Thom Lang/Alamy Images; 132 bottom: amybbb/Shutterstock, Inc.; 133 top: Image Source Plus/Alamy Images; 133 bottom left: Mondadori/Getty Images.

Maps by XNR Productions, Inc.